Jesus, Aramaic and Greek

JESUS, ARAMAIC & GREEK

G. R. Selby

BRYNMILL

copyright, ©, 1989, The Brynmill Press Ltd
ALL RIGHTS RESERVED

first published 1989
by
The Brynmill Press Ltd,
Cross Hill Cottage, Gringley-on-the-Hill,
Doncaster, South Yorkshire DN10 4RE England

typeset & printed by The Brynmill Press Ltd

I.S.B.N. 0 907839 40 1

CONTENTS

I The Background of the Aramaic Hypothesis	page 1
II The Aramaic Hypothesis	16
III Bilingualism and Palestine	32
IV The Gospels and the Aramaic Hypothesis	56
V Jesus and the Synagogue	82
VI The Use of Greek in the Post-Resurrection Period	93
VII Conclusion	104
Appendices	
A The Greek of the New Testament	108
B Analogies and Experiments in Bilingualism	110
C Aramaic Words as Used in the Gospels	114
D The Word *Ephphatha*	115
References	118

CHAPTER I

The Background of the Aramaic Hypothesis

In an age of apparently ever-increasing secularism, it is not always easy to appreciate what an important force in the history of the world the Christian Faith has been. It can be claimed justifiably that this Faith is the single most powerful force in the whole of human history. As both the cradle and the nursing mother of Western civilization, it is difficult accurately to assess its total impact upon human thought and behaviour. The least that can be said is that this influence and impact has been immense. It is, therefore, almost incredible that the cornerstone of this vast movement was a peasant Jew, Jesus of Nazareth. Because the name Jesus, closely associated with the title Christ, is so widely known throughout history and the contemporary world, it is often not sufficiently appreciated that virtually all that is known about "The Man" is contained within the pages of the New Testament and, more especially, those of the four Gospels.

It does not require, therefore, a great deal of reflection to realize how important the material found within the Gospels has been for the past. Of course, our present society is built upon the past, and so these documents have a contemporary importance for the part they have played in the historical development of all that might be described as Western culture. In addition, though, and equally important, is the major function the New Testament, and especially the

Gospels, have in the lives of millions of people throughout the world who still call themselves Christians.

Amongst many Christians, however, there exists a confusion concerning these documents. Not only is there uncertainty about the validity for late twentieth-century life of what these documents say, but also, the historical accuracy of that which is contained within the pages of the Gospels is often challenged. Paradoxically, this confusion arises not from a neglect of serious study of the documents, but rather from the immense amount of scholarly investigation which has been undertaken throughout this century. It can be claimed without fear of contradiction that no other books, or sets of documents, have been subject to such analysis, and even dissection, as have these, now ancient, documents.

The conclusions reached by New Testament scholars on the subjects of their chosen studies have been varied indeed. What is more, many of these studies have been both radical and reductionist. In other words, not only has the accuracy and truth of the contents of the New Testament been frequently questioned, but new, and often bizarre, interpretations have been suggested as being more accurate or realistic than that which has formerly been believed.

One of the most remarkable features of this plethora of New Testament investigation is the proliferation of hypotheses concerning the contents of these Scriptures. Rather more disturbing, though, is the habit which has developed amongst New Testament scholars of regarding these hypotheses, many of which are quite incapable of being realistically tested, as though they were proven fact. One such hypothesis, which is the main concern of this book, is what could be described as "The Aramaic Hypothesis".

This now widely accepted hypothesis can be approached by considering a passage from a near-contemporary book, written by a scholar of international repute. In 1974 the Dutch Roman Catholic scholar Edward Schillebeeckx published a book entitled *Jesus, an Experiment in Christology*. This book is described on the flap of the cover as "Schillebeeckx's life-work". When one considers the size of this book, which runs to over seven hundred and fifty pages, and which contains a vast amount of referential material, i.e. notes, technical information and bibliographies, that claim is easily accepted, and the extent of Schillebeeckx's diligent study appreciated.

Because our concern is with the Aramaic hypothesis, Schillebeeckx makes an important remark when he writes, "On historical grounds it is quite certain (despite some even very recent voices asserting that Jesus was bi-lingual) that he conveyed his message in Aramaic."[1] It has been pointed out above that an important contemporary concern is with the reliability of the New Testament. A student of this question might well, therefore, choose to consult such a book as *Can we Trust the New Testament?* published by J. A. T. Robinson in 1977. Here would be found a statement which supports Schillebeeckx's declaration. Robinson writes:

> Jesus certainly would have given his teaching in Aramaic, and so, except where the occasional word has been transliterated into Greek like *abba* (the child's word he used for addressing God as "Dad") we do not have any of his actual speech—and of course he didn't write anything himself.[2]

Similarly, a student pursuing this end might well wish to consult a biblical atlas to be informed of where the alleged Gospel events took place. If he consulted the *New Atlas of the Bible*, which is the work of another scholar of international repute, Jan H. Negenman, he might find the following passage. Negenman writes,

> At the beginning of our era, the divine revelation was conveyed to the world in the language of the Aramaen.

Students of the Greek New Testament try to explore the Aramaic background to the Scriptures, for the Christians of the Early Church not only spoke and wrote Aramaic, but thought in it too.[3]

Now when a reader comes across very similar statements upon the same subject, made by three acknowledged experts, he is apt to accept the truth of these statements without question. In so doing some significant implications of what is being said can easily be overlooked. For instance, if Robinson is right in what he says, that Jesus only spoke in Aramaic, the reader of an English version of the Gospels is immediately removed one stage further away from the words which Jesus actually spoke. This is because such a reader is not only dependent upon the person who translates from the original Greek of the New Testament into English, but is also dependent upon the hypothetical person who, Robinson would claim, first translated the Aramaic into Greek. It is, however, unfortunately a fact that translators can sometimes in their translations convey not what the original person spoke or wrote, but what the translator might think the author meant. A quotation from the New English Bible may illustrate this point. In chapter four, verse one of S*t* Paul's Epistle to the Galatians, the N.E.B. reads, "So long as the heir is a minor, he is no better off than a slave." Now this *may* have been what Paul intended, but it is certainly not what he wrote. Paul in this passage used a normal Greek word for *infant*, and whilst an infant is usually regarded as a minor, a minor is not always an infant. Hence the translator has written what he thought Paul meant, and not what he wrote, notwithstanding that Jewish ideas of minority were different from our own. Even more significant, though, are the words "he is no better off than a slave". Paul did not write this. He said that the heir does not differ from the slave in one important respect. Whilst he is an infant he is under guardians and stewards; that is, both heir and slave are alike under authority. The question of whether or not the heir is better off than the slave does not arise. The interpretation is both irrelevant and gratuitous.

Now the point is that if an English translator with, no doubt, the very best of intentions, can so change the meaning of St Paul's words, might it not be that the person who, allegedly, translated Jesus' words out of Aramaic into Greek similarly imposed his own interpretation? The statement that Jesus spoke only Aramaic, therefore, in itself raises the question of whether we can, in fact, trust the Gospels to be an accurate account of Jesus' words. If, on the other hand, it can be shown that some of Jesus' words were very probably spoken in the Greek in which they are recorded in the Gospels, we are brought one stage nearer to him.

It becomes apparent that it is important to cultivate a critical capacity. When certain implications of scholarly statements are so observed, in many cases the awareness of other implications soon follows. Another somewhat surprising fact about all three statements quoted above is that none of the three writers offer any evidence whatsoever for their quite sweeping claims. It is, perhaps, possible to excuse Robinson, for his book is a small paperback intended for a somewhat popular readership. In such a book it would not be easy to find space for evidential support for all the statements a writer might make. No such excuse, however, is possible for Schillebeeckx. As has been mentioned above, an important feature of Schillebeeckx's work is the immense amount of referential paraphernalia. In the main text of his thesis, which runs to six hundred and seventy pages, the author has over nine hundred references. In addition there are over ninety pages of "Notes and Technical Information", although, somewhat surprisingly, there is no subject index. There are also numerous passages scattered throughout the book which contain nothing but references to other books. Hence the lack of any evidence whatsoever for the dogmatic statement which Schillebeeckx makes that Jesus conveyed his message only in Aramaic is surprising to say the least.

What, however, is equally disturbing to the discriminating critic is that both Schillebeeckx and Robinson declare that it is quite certain that Jesus taught only in Aramaic. The question must be asked, "What kind of certainty can this be?" It may be supposed that there are some things which, given the regularity of the world in which we live, can be said to be certain. Arithmetically we can be sure that two and two will always make four. We can be certain that if the temperature of water is raised to a sufficient degree it will boil, and similarly, if it is lowered to a sufficient degree, it will freeze. Again, we can be certain that if an object held in the hand is released, it will invariably fall towards the ground. These are certainties which can continually be tested contemporaneously. However, even the truth of statements concerning other contemporary phenomena is far less certain.

Writing in the London *Daily Telegraph* of Thursday 22 January, 1987, Emeritus Professor H. Lipson of the University of Manchester Institute of Science and Technology declared that there is no finality (hence certainty) in scientific truth. He wrote, "In science there is no such finality; for example, Newton's theory of gravitation is now known to be only a close—a very close—approximation". Newton's theory (or hypothesis) of the law of gravitation can repeatedly be put to empirical testing. Even with this almost endless opportunity, Professor Lipson states that only a close approximation to the truth can be achieved. This alone must cast a degree of doubt upon both Schillebeeckx's and Robinson's claims to certainty.

At most, the best that can be said of even scientific empirical enquiry is that it can only provide, in most cases, an approximation to the truth. There can be little certainty. The next question which has to be faced is whether or not the Aramaic hypothesis is susceptible to empirical investigation. The statement that Jesus spoke only in Aramaic is a statement about a series of historical events; so a prior question has to be asked and answered, namely, the question of whether or not historical events are capable of being investigated and tested empirically.

A simple illustration demonstrates that they are not. I may make the statement that I was in London yesterday. This would be a statement concerning a very recent and particular, if unimportant, historical event. It can soon be shown, however, that there are no empirical means by which my statement can be tested. There are certain peripheral elements associated with my alleged historical claim which might be put to some empirical test. For instance, if I claim to have travelled by train, and if some railway employee could identify the ticket by which I allegedly travelled, my fingerprints might be found upon it. On the other hand I might have handled the ticket only when I was wearing gloves. What is more, in spite of what I claimed previously, I might have travelled to London by car. In that case the mileage of the car would have to be checked to see if that would permit such a journey of this length. That would mean, however, that the mileage prior to my alleged journey would have to be known. In any case I might have driven somewhere else, covering approximately the same mileage as would be required for a journey to and from London. The dust from my shoes might be analyzed to see if it corresponded with the dust of the streets of London, but it is obvious that, at best, this would provide only a certain amount of slight and limited circumstantial evidence.

Two other illustrations may demonstrate the immunity of historical events to empirical investigation; one of which is general, the other particular. First, if historical events were amenable to empirical testing, how much easier would be the task of the police in investigating crime! Circumstantial evidence, which can arise from empirical testing of certain peripheral aspects of the crime, is often suspect. Nothing can replace the information provided by witnesses. This, in itself, should offer us guidance concerning what is the right method in our approach to assessing the reliability, or otherwise, of the Aramaic hypothesis.

Turning our attention now to the particular illustration mentioned above, it will be seen that this concerns one of the most widely observed events in the history of the world. When President John F. Kennedy was assassinated in Dallas, there were thousands of witnesses present, and many millions more who saw the event on television. The historical fact that President Kennedy was shot to death is incontrovertible, and the fact that this event was captured on film provides an opportunity for empirical testing, which is not often available in respect of historical events. In spite of these most unusual circumstances, the evidence as to who fired the shot which killed the President was, and is, far less than certain.

It must be concluded, therefore, that the Aramaic hypothesis cannot be substantiated by empirical testing. That is not to say, however, that some of the evidence for the hypothesis may not be put to some real and adequate testing. The primary methods of investigation must, therefore, be those which are employed in any historical study. As much evidence as possible must be gathered together, examined with careful scrutiny, and tested by the methods proper to historiography. It should be self-evident that these methods are similar to those used in a court of law, and this fact has important implications. In an English court of criminal law, the evidence against the accused has to convince the jury beyond all reasonable doubt that the person is guilty. Both reason and history demonstrate that even when a jury has been convinced "beyond all reasonable doubt", they can still be wrong. There is little absolute certainty in a court of law, and similarly there is little absolute certainty in historical study. It is largely a matter of probability, and academic study is fatally flawed if those who undertake it do not realize that even their most treasured hypothesis may still be wrong. The most we can hope for is to form an opinion, based on the available evidence, that one state of affairs is more probable than another. With these points in mind it is, to say the least, unscholarly of both Schillebeeckx and Robinson to claim certainty for the Aramaic hypothesis.

Another important modern scholar makes a statement similar to those mentioned above. Thorleif Boman writes, "Jesus and the Apostles spoke Aramaic—unless Harris Birkeland should prove to be right in his hypothesis that Jesus and his Apostles spoke a folk dialect of Hebrew."[4] Again, like the scholars previously mentioned, Boman provides no evidence for his claim. Also, in his reference to Birkeland's hypothesis, Boman, like Schillebeeckx and Robinson, seems far from clear about what, in history, can, and cannot, be proved. The reference to an Hebrew dialect, however, may prove a useful starting point for a brief examination of the history of the development of the Aramaic hypothesis, for Birkeland is not the first to conjecture that Hebrew rather than Aramaic might be the language behind the Greek of the Gospels.

The seed-ground for the Aramaic hypothesis can be found in the later decades of the nineteenth century. Two developments may be said to have been significant in this respect. These two developments are the work which was done in what was commonly called "Lower Criticism", and in the increasing prominence given to the hypothesis of the priority of the Gospel according to S[t] Mark.

The task of "Lower Criticism" is the reconstruction of the text of the Bible. In respect of the New Testament, much work was done in this sphere, in the nineteenth century, by such great scholars as Constantius Tischendorf of Leipzig, B. F. Westcott and F. J. A. Hort, of Cambridge and London, and R. F. Weymouth, also of London. These were followed by such men as Eberhard Nestle, whose life and work stretched into the second decade of the twentieth century, J. Wellhausen, G. Dalman, and Erwin Nestle, the son of Eberhard. The senior Nestle's reconstruction of the text of the New Testament became accepted as a standard text, as did Erwin's revision of his father's work, which he published in 1949. Wellhausen, Eberhard Nestle, and, to a certain extent, Dalman, in reconstructing the text of the Gospel according to St Mark, from the best material available, came to the conclusion that the Greek of the Gospel is strongly coloured by an Aramaic tradition. On the other hand, Dr C. A. Briggs, Professor of Theological Encyclopaedia and Symbolics at the Union Theological Seminary, New York, and joint editor, with S. R. Driver and A. Plummer, of the International Critical Commentaries, published a book in 1904 in which he argued that an original Gospel written in Hebrew lay behind the Gospel according to St Mark.[5] Already, therefore, in the early years of this century, there was a difference of opinion regarding the language which might lie behind the Markan Gospel.

The claim of Nestle, Wellhausen and Dalman, that the Greek of the second Gospel had an Aramaic colouring, became more significant when taken in conjunction with the hypothesis of the primacy of this Gospel. For centuries the received opinion had been that the Gospel according to St Matthew was the primary work, and that the second Gospel was an abbreviated version of the first. However, more careful study indicated the strong probability that the second Gospel was the primary one. The hypothesis was then put forward that Mark first compiled a Gospel which became available to St Matthew and St Luke, who also had some other material in common (later to become known as "Q"), and, in addition, each had material peculiar to themselves. From these different materials the first and third Gospels were constructed.

It must be said that a careful study of this synoptic problem will reveal the reasonableness of this hypothesis. So widely accepted has this hypothesis become, however, that many scholars often appear to forget that it is still an hypothesis, for, instead, they tend to treat it as if it were an established and proven fact.

The progress of the hypothesis of the priority of Mark indicates how easily an hypothesis, which is quite incapable of proof or disproof, can gradually be accepted, not as an hypothesis, but as a certain fact. A serious problem arises when scholars who become convinced of the truth of a particular hypothesis, will countenance no questioning of it. This seems to have happened in the case of the Aramaic hypothesis. In one area at least, however, the hypothesis of the priority of Mark will retain its hypothetical status, because of the continued opposition of large sections of the Roman Catholic Church. Such a moderate and learned scholar as Xavier Léon Dufour can argue that

> Scholars are more and more coming to support the view that our three evangelists had access not to any long or well-constructed work, but to various collections of stories and sayings. This idea was originally put forward by (F. D.) Schleiermacher in 1817. This theory is very widely accepted nowadays as the most satisfactory explanation of the Synoptic problem.[6]

In spite of voices such as those of Dufour, however, the strength of the hypothesis of the priority of Mark has continued to grow apace. Accompanied by strong suggestions from the most eminent of New Testament textual scholars that there was an Aramaic flavour to the Greek of Mark, it is not difficult to see how further hypotheses developed and flourished. The Aramaic colouring soon became hypothetical documents, and then an hypothetical original Gospel. Having established the hypothesis that there might have been an Aramaic original of the Markan Gospel, it was not long before the idea of Aramaic originals was associated with other of the Gospels. From this position it is but a short step, knowing that Aramaic was a spoken language in Palestine at the time of Jesus, to the declaration that Jesus and his disciples spoke exclusively in Aramaic.

A considerable impetus was given to the belief in the existence and importance of the Aramaic background of the Gospels by the writing of C. C. Torrey. In his books *The Four Gospels* and *Our Translated Gospels*, neither of which is dated, Torrey argues strongly that there was an Aramaic original for the Gospel according to St Mark. Professor Torrey wrote a number of books in his long career. Two of his earliest were *Comparison of Ezra-Nehemiah* (1896), and *Ezra Studies* (1910). Torrey must have seemed extremely radical at the time, especially in his suggestion that Ezra was an entirely fictitious creation of the Chronicler, and that there was, in fact, no return of the exiles from Babylon. Most of Torrey's work was concerned with the Old Testament, and as late as 1928 he published a book entitled *The Second Isaiah*. This general direction of his studies, however, did not prevent him from publishing strong opinions about the background of the New Testament. He even went so far as to claim that an Aramaic source lies behind the first fifteen chapters of the Acts of the Apostles.

Other scholars, however, even decades after Torrey, were much less dogmatic in respect of this supposed Aramaic background. In his commentary on the Gospel according to St Mark, published in 1950, Dr Vincent Taylor writes,

> The Semitic background of Mark is unmistakable and the only questions for consideration are whether the Gospel is a translation of an Aramaic original, or whether the Greek suggests dependence on Aramaic tradition. ...W. F. Howard's judgement is in agreement with that of Lagrange: "His (Mark's) Greek is always Greek, yet translation Greek; not that he trans-

lates an Aramaic writing, but because he reproduces an Aramaic *katechesis*" (teaching).[7] ... More recently, M. Black has concluded a detailed study of the whole question with the opinion that "an Aramaic sayings-source or tradition lies behind the Synoptic Gospels," especially as regards the words of Jesus, but that "whether the source was written or oral, it is not possible from the evidence to decide."[8]

To recapitulate, it seems that in a little over half a century the following hypotheses were advanced: that behind the Gospel according to St Mark there was an Hebrew background or original (Briggs), or there was the folk-Hebrew dialect of Jesus and his followers (Birkeland), whatever that might have been; that the Greek of Mark has an Aramaic colouring (Wellhausen, Nestle and Dalman); that behind the Greek of Mark there is either an Aramaic tradition or an Aramaic original Gospel (Vincent Taylor); that there was an Aramaic original of the Gospel according to St Mark (Torrey); that the Markan Gospel is translation-Greek, and behind this is not an Aramaic writing but an Aramaic teaching. Going still further then is the argument of Black who would claim that an Aramaic sayings-source or tradition lies behind all the Synoptic Gospels; and, finally, it will be recalled, Torrey extends the Aramaic background to over half of the Acts of the Apostles.

Certain comments need to be made about these hypotheses. First, it is important to bear in mind that these *are* all hypotheses. Secondly, we note that there is no unanimity amongst these New Testament scholars. Thirdly, it is easy to see how hypotheses can and do proliferate. Fourthly, it is to be noted that some of these hypotheses are mutually exclusive, and finally, it is surprising how the Aramaic hypothesis can develop from that of an Aramaic colouring of the Greek of the Markan Gospel, to that of an Aramaic background of a major part of the New Testament.

This latter development is surprising, especially in view of what W. C. Allen, in his International Critical Commentary on the Gospel according to St Matthew, wrote as early as 1907. He said:

> I hope that the commentary has made clear the following facts about the editor of the book:
> (1) that he used St Mark's Gospel in Greek:
> (2) that he used a Greek translation of the Matthean Logia;
> (3) that he borrowed from a collection of Greek translations of Messianic passages from the Old Testament; [and]
> (4) that he had before him one or two narratives, in particular that of the centurion's servant, in a Greek form almost identical with the form in which they occur in the Third Gospel.[9]

Allen goes on to say that the personality of the author is completely enigmatic, and he would like to assume that this writer, writing as he does from entirely Greek sources, was a Jew of the Dispersion. However, Allen claims that the internal evidence of the Gospel will not permit such a conclusion. This Gospel, he argues, is a book of the Palestinian Church. On every page, he claims, there is the atmosphere of anti-Pharisaic Jewish Christianity. He argues that this Gospel is a counter-blast to the Jewish calumnies about Jesus; that official Judaism has rejected its Messiah, and in so doing has drawn down upon the nation the wrath of God, which will shortly be accomplished. Allen points out that the description of the Church is Palestinian, in that it still uses the Jewish nomenclature for its officials, and describes them as prophets, wise men and scribes. As it is for the Jewish church, so for the Christian Church offending members are to become as "heathen and toll-gatherers" (xviii. 17; Allen's translation). Allen argues that Jesus is portrayed as the Messiah who does not lift Jewish regulations, as the Second Gospel might suggest, in respect of divorce. (xix. 9) Indeed, he concludes, the whole Matthean Gospel is so interpenetrated with a Palestinian ethos, and so full of its ideas, that it could not have been written anywhere but on Palestinian soil.

This conclusion is of considerable interest and importance for this work, for Allen is convinced that his studies compel him to believe that the Gospel according to St Matthew was written by a Palestinian Christian Jew, who was not only Greek-speaking, but was greatly at ease in using Greek sources. If this is so, unless the author / editor of this Gospel did not speak Aramaic, he must have been a bilingual Jew of Palestine. The only doubt is whether or not he knew Aramaic, not whether or not he knew Greek. If this writer, obviously a prominent person in the Jewish-Christian Church of Palestine, was Greek speaking, it is difficult to see why other Jews, and Jesus himself, could not have been, similarly, Greek speaking, and bilingual. The following chapters will examine both the argument for the Aramaic hypothesis, and the evidence for bilingualism and even trilingualism in the land where Jesus lived, taught, died and rose again.

There is one further point which supports Allen's arguments. In Matthew x. 5, Jesus, when sending out the Twelve disciples on their mission, forbade them to go to the Gentiles. This is in accord with Allen's claim that Matthew sees Jesus as the Messiah, whose mission is to the Chosen People. Furthermore, the implication must be that the author of this Gospel must have believed that the disciples were able to communicate with the Gentiles, hence able to speak Greek, or there would have been little point in stating that Jesus made this prohibition.

CHAPTER II

The Aramaic Hypothesis

Behind the development of the Aramaic hypothesis, as described in the previous chapter, lay the belief that Aramaic was a spoken language in Palestine during the lifetime of Jesus. For this belief there is some considerable evidence. (See below, pp. 33 ff.) The question, however, as to whether or not this was the only language spoken in Galilee in the early years of the first century is an historical question of a very different order. Even if the majority of the people of Galilee, at that time, spoke only one language, that does not necessarily in itself demonstrate that Jesus was so confined. It is exceedingly difficult to ascertain just what languages a deceased person did, or did not, speak, as the following illustration will show.

Friends and former colleagues of the present writer may recall that he spent some little time in the remoter regions of Central America. The evidence they have of this is, first, they can remember his departure, and could offer to witness to this "historical event". Furthermore, they will recall what his absence involved for their own work-load, and they may also remember his return, and subsequent work with them. They have also, somewhat fortuitously, retained some letters and postcards received from him during his stay in Central America. They have heard him speak of his experiences there, and seen photographs which he took in the countries he visited. From what they have read and heard about these regions, they understand that, in the more remote areas, very little English is spoken. Now the

The Aramaic Hypothesis

question arises: "Could this sojourner in Central America speak Spanish?" The friends who are interested in this question cannot themselves speak Spanish. Apart from the occasional Spanish word which they remember hearing their friend use, but which, on the other hand, might have been picked up during a week's package tour in Spain, they never heard him speak Spanish. Now, supposing that whilst these people were trying to discover whether or not their friend spoke Spanish, he suddenly died. It would then be exceedingly difficult to decide whether or not their friend had this facility. On the one hand the evidence suggests that he could speak the language, because, it seems, he was able to get along quite satisfactorily in an area where it can be demonstrated Spanish is universally spoken, and little English is known. But this is the extent of their positive knowledge. Someone else could create the hypothesis that their friend, during his stay in Central America (a) had an interpreter, or (b) managed to survive with a few Spanish words, a Spanish–English dictionary, and a considerable expertise in sign language. It would be extremely difficult to prove that their deceased friend could speak Spanish, or, for that matter, that he could not. To come to a decision they would have to weigh the evidence; but at best this would only achieve a degree of probability in one direction or another. Of course, if the matter was sufficiently important to them, they could, at considerable expense, go to those parts of Central America which their friend visited, accompanied by someone who was fluent in Spanish, and search for some persons who could remember their friend's visit, and who could witness to his ability, or inability, to speak their language. Even if they were able to do this, and to find such people, they would still have to make a judgement concerning the reliability of their new acquaintances as witnesses. Whatever else may be its value, this analogy at least demonstrates the limitations imposed upon such a quest, even in a near contemporary situation. How much greater the difficulty, therefore, when the field of investigation is a matter of ancient history!

The second basis for the Aramaic hypothesis is the claim that the Greek texts of the Gospels imply Aramaic originals. This is really the heart of the hypothesis, and the evidence for this claim needs to be examined most carefully. Before this work is done, however, two other points need to be made. The first is that it must be remembered—and, in the present climate of New Testament study, this fact cannot be reiterated too frequently—that the claim that Jesus gave his teaching entirely in Aramaic is only a conjecture, an hypothesis. In spite of the overwhelming conviction of the majority of New Testament scholars that it is a proven fact that Jesus spoke only Aramaic, it is not, because it is simply not possible to prove such an historical assertion. Therefore, the conjectural basis of the Aramaic hypothesis must continually be kept in mind. As has been demonstrated above, there are no means by which this hypothesis may be put to any empirical test. The only means of investigation available to the students of this question are procedures similar to those used in a court of law. The evidence for and against the hypothesis must be revealed as clearly and unambiguously as possible. Then a conclusion must be reached which is based on the evidence, not upon previously entrenched positions, and which does not claim greater freedom from doubt then the evidence permits.

The second point is that the rejection of the Aramaic hypothesis does not involve the denial of the historical claim that Aramaic was a spoken language in Palestine at the time when Jesus lived. Nor would such a rejection imply that Jesus did not himself speak Aramaic. On the contrary; both these claims are readily admitted by the present writer. What is being questioned are the hypotheses that (a) Jesus and his disciples spoke only Aramaic, and (b) the belief that there is some evidence that the Greek of the New Testament is based upon elements of Aramaic, and that this pheno-

THE ARAMAIC HYPOTHESIS

menon demonstrates that hence Aramaic Christian documents are the basis of our Greek Gospels.

It will be seen that the Aramaic hypothesis is not one, but a collection of hypotheses which lean on one another. Indeed, the apparent strength of the Aramaic hypothesis is obtained from the apparent support which one hypothesis gives to another. Whether, in fact, they do so support one another remains to be ascertained. Furthermore, as in the case of the hen and the egg, it is not easy to decide which hypothesis came first. It could be that the belief that Aramaic was the only language spoken in Galilee at the time of Our Lord provided the impetus for the textual investigation which allegedly produced the evidence of the Aramaic base of the Greek Gospels. Or, of course, it could have been the other way round.

The evidence for the claim that Aramaisms underlie the Greek of the Gospels can be stated, examined and assessed much more concisely than can the evidence for the claim that Jesus and his disciples spoke only Aramaic. As the former of these two claims has been the one which has exercised such great influence upon contemporary New Testament study, it is appropriate that the examination of this claim be made first of all.

It is frequently stated by New Testament scholars that the evidence for the Aramaisms underlying the Greek of the Gospels is so technically complex that only those who are experts in Aramaic are capable of assessing and judging the evidence. But this is professional arrogance, and obscurantism. If the case for the hypothesis has a sound basis, it should be possible for it to be expressed in such a way that any competent scholar can assess its truth, or otherwise. Such a description of the arguments for the hypothesis that Aramaisms underlie the Greek of the Gospels is expressed very lucidly by Joachim Jeremias in the first volume of his *New Testament Theology*.[10] This description will here be used as the basis of the hypothesis, and will be described and assessed.

Jeremias begins his presentation by admitting that what he claims to be the nearest linguistic analogies to the sayings of Jesus are in popular Aramaic passages of the Palestinian Talmud and Midrashim which have their home in Galilee, but did not attain written form until between the fourth and sixth centuries A.D. This might seem a somewhat slender claim from which to begin a defence of this part of the Aramaic hypothesis, or a claim for the Aramaic basis of the *logia* of Jesus in the Synoptic Gospels, as Jeremias so describes it. There is some evidence that written Aramaic was at a low ebb during the lifetime of Jesus, and immediately afterwards, and that it experienced a resurgence in the second century. This will be discussed later (see p. 99). If there was but little Aramaic written in the first half of the first century, then Jeremias' arguments are indeed perilously based.

Jeremias' next conclusion, however, that Galilean Aramaic differed in pronunciation from that of Southern Palestine does little to advance the strength of his base, for the only evidence he can give for this assumption is Matthew xxvi.73 (when Peter, outside the High Priest's palace after the arrest of Jesus, is accused of being one of his disciples because "your accent betrays you"). In fact this text is not evidence for the Aramaic hypothesis at all; rather, Jeremias' point is a conclusion which is expressly based upon the Aramaic hypothesis. It is, indeed, a fine example of the circular argument. It is entirely possible that the Greek *patois* was pronounced differently in the north from the south, and this would equally well explain the Matthean text. It is, of course, possible that Simon Peter was speaking in Aramaic, but there is no evidence that he was so speaking strong enough to make this text the basis for the Aramaic hypothesis, as Jeremias attempts to do.

The heart of Jeremias' argument for the Aramaic basis for

the *logia* of Jesus is a list of twenty-six words which, he claims, are to be found on the lips of Jesus. These words, Jeremias argues, are in addition to place names, personal names, and designations of descent or groups. As Jeremias places a good deal of importance upon these twenty-six words, it is appropriate to assess their significance very carefully, although it might be thought that a group of twenty-six words out of all those which Jesus is reported as using in the Synoptic Gospels does not constitute a very convincing foundation for so far-reaching an hypothesis.

A careful examination of this list of twenty-six words, however, reveals an even more slender basis. It should be remembered that Jeremias speaks of his study as the *logia* of the *Synoptic* Gospels. It is, therefore, somewhat surprising to find that eight of these words are nowhere to be found in the Synoptic Gospels. The reader is apt to be puzzled by this until it is recalled that Jeremias has a *penchant* for discovering "non-canonical sayings of Jesus". Jeremias, in fact, gives the source of these eight words as "rabbinic tradition". Another word which Jeremias claims to be found on Jesus' lips is reported only by Jerome. We are therefore left with a maximum of seventeen indisputably New Testament words. One of these words, however, is in St John i. 42–3, and is the name, Cephas. This, it would seem, should be disqualified from inclusion in Jeremias' list on two counts. First, of course, it is not of the *logia* of the *Synoptic* Gospels, and, secondly, it is a proper name, which Jeremias previously seems to have claimed to have excluded.

In respect of this claim, however: of the remaining sixteen words of Aramaic which Jeremias claims to find on the lips of Jesus, seven, by any description, appear to be proper names. They are: *Abba, Beelzebul, Gehenna* (surely a place-name in origin), *Passover, Sabbath, Satan* and *Mammon*. Of these words, *Passover, Sabbath* and *Satan*, and another of the remaining nine words, *rabbi*, must have been transliterated into Greek for centuries before Jesus was born.

They are such technical terms that it is quite illicit of Jeremias to claim any special function for them in Jesus' conversation.

Of the remaining nine words which Jeremias claims to find on the lips of Jesus, two occur in the command of Jesus to Jairus's daughter. Two more of these words are words from the Cross, and two more appear in "Bar Jona" and "Boanerges" although, in respect of the last two words, it might not appear unjust to suggest that they are names also. We are therefore left with three words, *rabbi*, which has already been mentioned, *sata*, meaning a measure, and *raca*, a word of abuse. In respect of the word *raca*, used in Matthew v. 22, it should be pointed out that it is immediately followed by the Greek word *more*, for which there is no Aramaic equivalent. This fact caused W. C. Allen[11] to suggest that this Greek word was adoped into use by the Aramaic-speaking population. There is no need to stress, however, that Allen's comment here is of the same order as Jeremias' comment on Matthew xxvi. 73. It could be that the Aramaic term of abuse was adopted into the Greek *patois*. Students of bilingualism would point out that this would be the more normal pattern. For instance, many bilingual Welshmen, when speaking English, will interpose a Welsh word of abuse. Whichever was the adopting language, the word *moros* linked with *raca* is, in itself, evidence of bilingualism in the environment of Jesus. It is also interesting to note that the word *moros* is common in the Septuagint, but occurs in the New Testament only in S[t] Matthew and the Pauline epistles. Other than the word *sata*, therefore, Jeremias is left with only one authentic Aramaic word (and that a swear-word) on the lips of Jesus, apart from the words from the Cross, those from the episode in the house of Jairus, and names, or designations of descent or groups. As with the case of the linguistic analogies, and the claim that the pronunciation of Galilean Aramaic differed from that of Southern Palestine, the foundation which these

Aramaic words provide seems a precarious one for such a large edifice.

Jeremias continues his argument with a section on "Ways of speaking preferred by Jesus". It is important to submit this section to careful analysis. He begins this part of his study with a discussion of the linguistic device called "the divine passive". In respect of this, Jeremias writes:

> Even in the pre-Christian period there was a prohibition against uttering the tetragrammaton, to ensure that the second commandment (Ex. xx. 7, Deut. v. 11) was followed as scrupulously as possible and to exclude any misuse of the divine name. Later on, but still in the pre-Christian period, there arose the custom of speaking of God's actions and feelings in *periphrases*. Jesus certainly had no hesitation in using the word "God", but to a large extent he followed the custom of the time and spoke of the action of God by means of circumlocutions.[12]

Jesus, therefore, used the divine passive frequently. Indeed Jeremias says, "The divine passive occurs round about a hundred times in the sayings of Jesus."[13] He goes on to say, "It is one of the clearest characteristics of his way of speaking."[14] It is important to note these two statements which Jeremias makes about Jesus' use of the "divine passive", for then he goes on to say that "The astonishing thing is that this phenomenon is almost completely absent from Talmudic literature." Jeremias is therefore pointing out that Jesus' use of the "divine passive" is in direct contrast to the use of Talmudic literature. He then goes on to say that "the general restraint in the use of the passive which is characteristic of Aramaic is alien to Greek."

It is not clear whether or not Jeremias realizes what he is saying. It may be that the expression of this conclusion in the negative way concealed the implications of the argument from Jeremias. What he is really saying, and this can be seen clearly if his conclusions are expressed in a positive rather than a negative fashion, is that the use of the "divine passive" is extremely rare in Talmudic literature, and also, in fact, in Aramaic generally. On the other hand, the use of the "divine passive" in Greek is extremely common. Jeremias emphasizes that the use of the "divine passive" is one of Jesus' most characteristic ways of speaking; he uses this device some one hundred times. In spite of his own findings and conclusion, Jeremias fails to see what they imply. The implication can only be that either Jesus was speaking in Aramaic in a most unusual way, or else he was speaking in Greek.

Jeremias points out that the "divine passive" is prominent in the literature of the Diaspora, and in the letters of Paul, all, of course, written in Greek, and he thinks that the Septuagint may be partly responsible for the use there. He quite properly rejects the notion that this phenomenon is to be attributed to secondary editorial activity. He then begins to argue, fairly confidently, that the solution lies in the use of the "divine passive" in apocalyptic literature, but his confidence tends to wane, for he goes on to say that "Jesus accords to the 'divine passive' an incomparably greater place than it is given in apocalyptic."[15] Jeremias omits to point out that apocalyptic writing arose during the Greek period in Palestine. It is difficult to resist the conclusion, in spite of Jeremias' failure to recognize it, that the answer to the apparent problem of the use of the "divine passive" by Jesus is that he was speaking Greek.

Jeremias' next step in this search for evidence of Aramaic lying behind the Greek of the New Testament is to discuss the matter of antithetic parallelism. Here, however, it has to be stated that Jeremias is most tentative in his argument, and appears not to be at all sure whether or not this really has any significance for the Aramaic hypothesis. He admits[16] that even to get this parallelism in a translation of the text into Aramaic he must first tamper with the Greek text.

He then goes on to say:

> Unfortunately, any verdict on the use of antithetic parallelism in the sayings of Jesus is made more difficult by the lack of any comprehensive investigation of Semitic antithetic parallelism. In particular, we are still completely in the dark about the extent to which it was used in the environment of Jesus.[17]

In other words, Jeremias confesses that no one really knows if antithetic parallelism was a characteristic of Aramaic at the time of Jesus. Jeremias further qualifies his position by pointing out that Jesus' use of this device is the exact opposite of its use in the Old Testament. Once more the precariousness of the evidence for this hypothesis is very apparent.

There is then, thirdly, in this section of Jeremias' work, an investigation of the use of rhythm in the speech of Jesus. Jeremias proceeds to identify four types of rhythmic sayings which, he claims, Jesus used. These four types are the two-beat, the three-beat, the four-beat and the *kina* metre. He then deals with each type separately. Before investigating Jeremias' examination of these rhythmic sayings, it would perhaps be helpful to indicate, as Jeremias allows, that C. F. Burney previously identified three of these rhythms, the four-beat, the three-beat and the *kina*, when he translated the sayings of Jesus from Greek into Aramaic. Jeremias claims to have discovered the two-beat rhythm, but there is a real question as to whether or not the two-beat rhythms have any relevance to the Aramaic argument.

Jeremias begins by pointing out that the speeches with the two-beat rhythms convey the central ideas of Jesus' teaching. He suggests that the bulk of the teaching Jesus gave to the general public at large would have been dominated by speech with this rhythm. But any value this has for the Aramaic hypothesis is greatly damaged when Jeremias has to admit that the two-beat rhythm is just as evident in the Greek text as it is in an Aramaic translation of the Greek text. Jeremias points out that the commission with which the Disciples are sent out (Matthew x. 8) rhymes in an Aramaic translation of the Greek, but then it also rhymes in the Greek original. As the two-beat rhythm, and in Matthew x. 8 the rhyme also, is there in the Greek, it can only mean that these central ideas of Jesus' teaching to the public are just as likely to have been given in Greek as in Aramaic. That is the only conclusion possible from a study of this particular rhythmic material. It remains to be seen whether other kinds of evidence may not tilt the balance of probability towards the conclusion that this teaching was, in fact, in Greek. It is also significant that Jeremias makes only two two-beat-sayings translations into Aramaic. These are part of Matthew x. 8, and are the words *dorean elabete* and *dorean dote*. He chooses, therefore, to translate only three words of these two-beat rhythmic sayings, one of which, *dote*, occurs only once in the New Testament.

His treatment of the four-beat, three-beat and *kina* rhythms, however, is in sharp contrast, for here his translations into Aramaic are quite extensive. It can be assumed, therefore, that the heart of the linguistic case for the Aramaic hypothesis should be found in what is said of these kinds of rhythmic sayings.

Jeremias admits that the contexts of the four-beat sayings are different from those of the two-beat. Indeed, he says:

> It is hardly a coincidence that many sayings with four-beat lines are addressed to the inner circle of followers and the messengers, for the most part giving instructions but also bringing consolation. The four-beat line is pre-eminently the rhythm for the *instruction of disciples*. [his italics][18]

The intent of this present thesis is not to deny that Jesus spoke, and indeed at times taught, in Aramaic. It is the

Aramaic hypothesis that is being challenged: i.e. that Jesus spoke exclusively in Aramaic, and that there were Aramaic originals which formed the basis for the Greek Gospels. On the contrary, if Jesus was bilingual it would be entirely natural for him to speak Aramaic within the confines of his own group of disciples. Aramaic would be the "home" language of the disciples, as it was, most probably for Jesus. If an Aramaic original lies behind these sayings which in translation have a four-beat rhythm this, taken in conjunction with our conclusion about the two-beat rhythm discussed above, would tend to support the argument that Jesus was bilingual, rather than denying it. It should be pointed out in passing, however, that an "Aramaic" original lying behind the Greek of the Gospels does not necessarily imply that Aramaic originals of the Gospels were ever in existence. This will be discussed in more detail later.

Jeremias gives eleven instances of the three-beat rhythmic sayings. Of these, seven are peculiar to Matthew, three have parallels in Luke, and one appears only in Luke. Again, the contexts of these sayings are different from those of the other two sets of rhythmic sayings. The three-beat rhythm is used, Jeremias claims, "to drive home important sayings and maxims". A number of instances which he gives are from the Sermon on the Mount. Now, in much of his teaching, Jesus is evidently taking sayings and maxims already known to some of his hearers, and giving to these sayings his own touch of originality. There is nothing improbable in the suggestion that Jesus knew these sayings in their original Aramaic form, and himself translated them into Greek for the greater part of his audience to understand more easily. Again, there is nothing inconsistent in this suggestion with Jeremias' own conclusion that "much of the rhythmic language was lost when the sayings were translated into Greek."[19] Jesus was not translating for posterity, but was translating in order that he might best convey his own message in the language most widely understood by his hearers. This is, at least, a reasonable presumption. Again, the claim that much of the rhythmic language was lost in translation (a hypothesis in itself) argues just as strongly for the bilingualism of Jesus as against it, for the ability to speak Greek by no means implies the ability to translate into a Greek of high quality.

When Jeremias goes on to give a review of the *kina* metre, he describes it as having "the most individual rhythm: 3 + 2 with occasional variations of 2 + 2 and 4 + 2." He says, "It derives from the lament for the dead (*kina*), in which the singer who leads the lament utters a long cry (three-beat) to which the lamenting women make answer with a shorter echo (two-beat)."[20] Jeremias gives nine examples but, rather confusingly, says that "in one passage in the gospels, we find Jesus taking up a real *kina*." The text is given as Luke xxiii. 21, but this is an error, and should read Luke xxiii. 31 ("If they do this when the wood is green, what will happen when it is dry?") He says that the *kina* metre serves above all "to express *strong inner emotion*." [his italics] As the "real *kina*" is Jesus' words to the grieving women on his way to crucifixion, it does not seem surprising that his speech should have been expressed in this metre.

Jeremias says that the *kina* metre "covers a wide span, including laments, warnings, threats, admonitions and summons as well as beatitudes and messages of salvation."[21] However, the examples he gives do not seem, quite, to relate closely to this catalogue. When the eight other examples he gives of *kina* are examined, the most striking element of comparison is that at least five of these sayings are by no means necessarily original to Jesus. They are:

(1) the children's sing-song (Matthew xi. 17, par. Luke vii. 32);

(2) "By your standard of measure it will be measured to you" (Mark iv. 24 and pars.);

(3) "He who is not with me is against me" (Matthew xii. 30; Luke xi. 23);

(4) "The last shall be first and the first last" (Matthew xx. 16);

(5) "For where the carcase is there also will the vultures be gathered" (Matthew xxiv. 28—not 48 as Jeremias gives it; par. Luke xvii. 37)

The other three are similarly aphoristic sayings. They are: "For whoever wishes to save his life shall lose it, but whoever loses his life for my sake and the gospel's shall save it " (Mark viii. 35); "Render to Caesar the things that are Caesar's" (Mark xii. 17) and "Do not think that I came to abolish the Law or the prophets: I did not come to abolish but to fulfil." (Matthew v. 17)

Jeremias concludes his discussion of the rhythmic sayings with the comment, "A comparison of the parallel traditions shows that much of this rhythmic language was lost when the sayings were translated into Greek." This is, no doubt, true; but the loss of these rhythms says nothing about when the translations were made, or by whom. It is just as possible that the rhythms were lost if and when Jesus himself translated them, as if they were translated by members of the early Church.

Jeremias' final section of "Ways of Speaking Preferred by Jesus" deals with alliteration, assonance and paronomasia. Concerning these, Jeremias has little more to say than to remark that when the sayings of Jesus are translated back into Aramaic, they display an unusual degree of these phenomena. This would still be true if, as has been suggested above, the translations were made by Jesus himself.

Throughout the remainder of Jeremias' book there are frequent translations of the Greek text into Aramaic, many of which are claimed as the original texts. This, of course, is still conjectural, for no such originals now exist, if they ever did. Jeremias, for instance, gives a plausible translation into Aramaic of the Lord's Prayer, in the Lukan version. He says, "We have been brought to see that the Greek text is based upon an earlier Aramaic one."[22] But the reason why "we have been brought to see" this is the rhythm of the

Aramaic translation. In other words the principles described above provide the basis for all Jeremias' arguments for Aramaic originals. The strength of his argument depends upon the strength of these principles. As has been pointed out, some, for example the use of the "divine passive" and the two-beat rhythm, are exceedingly questionable in the support they are alleged to give to the claim of an Aramaic base.

Furthermore, throughout the book, in translations quoted from other sources as well as his own, there is seen an intrusive theological element. Aramaic translations are given to improve or amend the sense of the received text. Whilst this may be entirely legitimate from an hermeneutical point of view, in respect of the Aramaic hypothesis it is merely supporting one conjecture by another conjecture.

If Jeremias' presentation in these sections of his "New Testament Theology" is a fair, comprehensive and concise statement of the evidence upon which the Aramaic hypothesis is based, then the hypothesis is by no means as firmly based as its proponents have claimed. It is evident that Vincent Taylor's summing up of the Aramaic background to the Gospels is as far as the evidence permits anyone to go; indeed, his summing up may be too optimistic. Taylor writes:

> We have very good reason to speak of an Aramaic background to the Greek of the Gospel [Mark]; there are grounds for suspecting the existence of Aramaic sources, which may, however, be oral; we can speak of a tradition which is ultimately Aramaic; but to say more is speculation.[23]

After the above analysis of Jeremias' arguments, even this moderate statement by Vincent Taylor may be not without its element of speculation.

As has been emphasized above, the evidence for the Aramaic hypothesis (or hypotheses) is based on (a) the assumption that Aramaic was universally and, in Galilee, exclusively used at the time of Jesus, and (b) that the text of the Gospels implies that Aramaic originals existed upon which the Greek of the Gospels is based. It is evident that as (a) concerns historical events, that part of the hypothesis cannot be put to any empirical testing. Its validity or truth must be assessed in the light of other historical evidence. In respect of (b) some empirical testing is possible. Jeremias has provided the material evidence. In this chapter this evidence has been put to whatever testing is possible and appropriate. In view of this it can only be said that such items of evidence as the linguistic analogies with popular Aramaic passages of the Palestinian Talmud and Midrashim, the question of different pronunciations of Aramaic, the Aramaic words used by Jesus in the Gospels, the use of the "divine passive", the two-beat rhythms in the language of the Gospels, and the question of antithetic parallelisms, do not, individually, unquestionably support the thesis concerning the existence of Aramaic originals. On the contrary, some of these elements, notably the use of the "divine passive" and the two-beat rhythms, suggest that the originals of these were Greek. The other elements, that is, the four-beat rhythms, the three-beat rhythms, and the *kina* metre, the use of alliteration, assonance and paronomasia, and the random translations of some of the Greek text, do suggest an Aramaic background. It is exceedingly likely that Jesus did speak Aramaic in many situations, but that it did depend upon the contexts. The evidence given by Jeremias is by no means strong enough to compel belief in Aramaic original documents, or that Jesus spoke only Aramaic. On the contrary, much of this evidence is supportive of the hypothesis that Jesus was bilingual. The remainder of this work will be occupied with the search for evidence which might support this alternative hypothesis.

CHAPTER III

Bilingualism and Palestine

It is apparent from the discussion in the previous chapter that much of the alleged linguistic evidence for the Aramaic hypothesis arises from translating the Greek text of the Gospels into Aramaic. This, at best, can only be a kind of secondary evidence. The more primary linguistic evidence is to be found in what Jeremias describes as "the Aramaic basis of the *logia* of Jesus in the Synoptic Gospels". It is, therefore, important that these *logia* should be examined in more detail than has already been undertaken. The hypothesis from which this work begins, however, is that Jesus and his disciples were bilingual in Greek and Aramaic. It is even possible that Jesus and perhaps some of the disciples were trilingual and had some knowledge of Hebrew also. If the bilingual hypothesis can be given substantial support from available historical evidence it will be most important to consider these *logia* of Jesus, and in particular his use of Aramaic words, against this trilingual background. Consequently, the next step in this discussion will be the compilation and examination of the historical evidence for bilingualism in Palestine, in conjunction with a description of the phenomenon of bilingualism in general.

The general scholarly opinion about the language situation in Palestine in the early years of the Christian or Common era is easily and quickly summarized. It is that Hebrew had declined and almost disappeared as a language spoken by ordinary people, and that it had become the language of the scholar, in some ways not dissimilar to the position of

Latin in the Western Europe of the late Middle Ages. Aramaic had taken its place as the language of ordinary communication, universally amongst the Jews of the Holy Land. Of the position of Greek, and of the extent of its use in Palestine, very little is said. Little also is said about the evidence for these assumptions. Furthermore, in so much biblical, and especially New Testament study, Aramaic has acquired an aura of sanctity, which implies that this language had attained a position in the estimation of the Jewish people only a little inferior to that of Hebrew. Again, no evidence is supplied for this assumption. When the evidence is examined, however, it is quickly apparent that the situation was by no means as simple as that which contemporary New Testament scholarship has assumed.

First of all it is worth reiterating that both Hebrew and Aramaic are ancient Semitic languages. There are ancient Hebrew inscriptions dating from the twelfth century B.C., and Aramaic inscriptions dating from the late tenth century, or at least the early ninth century B.C. It can be demonstrated that the two languages co-existed in Palestine for several centuries, before Aramaic developed the dominant position. Evidence of bilingualism in Palestine dates back to c. 700 B.C., as the episode between Hezekiah king of Judah and Rabshakeh, emissary of king Sennacherib of Assyria, recorded in 2 Kings xviii. 19ff. demonstrates. Rabshakeh had been declaring the message of the king of Assyria in Hebrew, but Hezekiah's representatives, Eliakim and Jo'ah reply: "Pray speak to your servants in the Aramaic language, for we understand it; do not speak to us in the language of Judah within the hearing of the people who are on the wall."(26) But Rabshakeh refused, and continued to cry out "in the language of Judah", that is, in Hebrew. This episode would suggest that Aramaic was at that time the language of the Court, the language of diplomacy, for the court officials of Judah understood it, whereas the ordinary people did not.

It should be remembered that language is not something that exists in a vacuum. The dominance of a language is almost always related to the dominance of the people whose language it basically is. In the phenomenon of bilingualism, it seems that it is the language of the dominant political power which prevails, whilst the language of the people whose political power is fading also declines; declines, but does not necessarily disappear. Such local languages often continue in the home, in literature, and especially in religion and worship. As Judah moved more and more into the hegemony of the great Eastern neighbouring power, whether it were Assyria, Babylonia or Persia, so the common language of the super-power gained increasing dominance at the expense of Judah's own language. Similar developments can be seen in other instances of bilingualism. The Welsh language declined under the dominance of the language of the dominant power, England. Welsh, however, did not disappear, although at times it seemed that it might. It became, very frequently, the language of the home, of literature, especially of poetry (notably in the Eisteddfod) and also, the language of the Chapel, which seemed to many Welsh people a much more indigenously Welsh institution than the somewhat Anglicized Church (later the Church in Wales). There is also an interesting comparison with the fate of German in the United States of America. In the 1830's and 1840's attempts were made to set up German-speaking States within the Union. During this period these efforts took political form. Colonies of German-speaking settlers were established in several Western territories with a view to creating a truly German region. The attempt failed, but many of these families and their descendants for several generations continued to be bilingual. Anti-German sentiment during the First World War swept away the props of German America: the German language press and the German language schools. But the pertinacity of a minority language is indicated by the experience of the present writer. In a very Anglicized and even Anglophile area of North Carolina, where the vast majority of family names, even of the Black population, are either English or Welsh, a small enclave of German Lutheran farmers survived, prospered, and maintained in their bilingualism the use of the German language in the home and in their worship until well into the second half of this century.

Aramaic, in Palestine, certainly became the dominant partner in the bilingual situation there. It may have reached its most dominant position soon after 400 B.C. The fact, as Meyers and Strange point out, that "the authors of Daniel and Ezra composed roughly half of these books in Aramaic" is "a testimony to the strong position of this language" after that date.[24] Meyers and Strange also point to the papyri found in a cave in the Wadi Daliyeh. It seems that this cave was the last refuge for important Samarian families fleeing before the impending conquest of Alexander the Great. These people were overtaken and slaughtered, men, women and children; but the papyri, which were apparently very important to the refugees, survived. Meyers and Strange say,

> They were almost all legal or administrative in nature, and they were in Aramaic. All were written in the province and/or city of Samaria. Many of the names preserved in them are Yahwistic (they contain "*iah*" (Yhwh) at the end or "*Je*" (Yhwh) at the beginning). It is significant that these papyri appear in Aramaic, not Hebrew. Nevertheless, one seal is inscribed in Paleo-Hebrew script and in the Hebrew language. It reads, "Yahu, son of [San]ballat, governor of Samaria". We see that Hebrew still functions as a minor public, or official language, but that Aramaic is by far the dominant tongue.[25]

These scholars also refer to the recent discoveries of

mainly Aramaic ostraca from the South of Palestine, at Khirbet el Kôm, from the third century B.C., and this is further indication of the extent of the use of Aramaic. But, inevitably, the language of the dominant power becomes the dominant language in the bilingual or even trilingual situation. In a general comment upon the three languages, Hebrew, Aramaic and Greek, Meyers and Strange say, "The evidence seems overwhelming, then, that Aramaic was far more widely used in Palestine than Hebrew, although it *did not reach the breadth of the use of Greek.*" (my italics) This is what should be expected, particularly if what has been observed concerning other instances of bilingualism hold true for this bilingual/trilingual situation.

New Testament scholars seem to have had a predilection to believe that the Jews of Jesus' day had some religious and/or political affection for the Aramaic language. It is difficult to see on what evidence this assumption is based. Aramaic was the language of invaders, and especially the language of the invader who brought about that most traumatic experience of the people of Judah, the Babylonian destruction of the Temple, and the Exile. It was also the official language of the Persian Empire and, after the reign of Cyrus, the Jews had comparatively little cause for regarding the Persians with affection. Aramaic was a means of communication, and had none of the sacred associations of Hebrew. There is little cause to suppose that Jews would wish to adhere to this language when another language was a much more efficient means of communication in the world at large. It might be argued that there could be antipathies towards the Greek language, for this too was the language of an invader; but to claim this would be to ignore the evidence. It can amply be demonstrated that a significant number of Jews throughout the Hellenistic and Roman periods found Hellenism a considerable attraction. It is true that the production of the Septuagint was, no doubt, an act of realistic appreciation of the situation of the world at large, but there must surely be some significance in the fact that a careful rendering of the Scriptures into Greek was achieved by about 275 B.C., whilst it was not until the Christian era that a similar translation was achieved into Aramaic. The earliest of the Targums may have made their appearance in the first century of the Christian era, but these were free, even paraphrastic renderings into popular Aramaic, and their dates are more likely to be towards the end of the second century A.D. The Syrian (Peshitta) version probably appeared at the end of the second century also, but, in any case, this was not the kind of Aramaic spoken in Palestine.

A hint may be found in the Mishnah, for example, that in some quarters Aramaic was not even regarded as a respectable language. In Yadaim iv.5 it says, "The [Aramaic] version that is in Ezra and Daniel renders the hands unclean," but it seems that the problem was with the script rather than with the language itself, for this section concludes with the words, "[The Holy Scriptures] render the hands unclean only if they are written in the Assyrian character, on leather, and in ink."

The only other reference to the Aramaic language in the Mishnah is in Shekalim v.3 which reads,

> There were four seals in the Temple and on them was inscribed "Calf", "Kid", "Sinner", "Ram". Ben Azzai says; There were five and on them was inscribed in Aramaic "Calf", "Ram", "Kid", "Poor sinner", and "Rich sinner".

Lest this should appear to suggest, however, that Aramaic had a small but special place in the Temple, it is as well to remember that the Mishnah also says, in the same book, Shekalim, that "In three baskets, each holding three seals, did they take up *Terumah* out of the Shekel-chamber, and on them was inscribed [the letters] *Aleph*, *Beth*, and *Gimel*. R. Ishmael says, 'On them was inscribed in Greek [the letters] *Alpha, Beta,* and *Gamma.*'" So it is evident that whatever place was afforded to Aramaic was also given to Greek. In Megillah i. 8 it says, "Rabban Simeon b Gamaliel says: The Books [of Scripture] too, they have only permitted to be written in Greek," (as well as Hebrew, of course). In Sotah ix. 14 it says, "During the war of Titus they [the Sages] forbade the crowns of the brides and that a man should teach his son Greek." This Titus, of course, refers to the son of Vespasian, who was the destroyer of Jerusalem in A.D. 70. So this prohibition of Greek was almost forty years after the Crucifixion of Jesus, and, in any case, the prohibition would hardly have been necessary if Jewish fathers were not teaching their sons Greek.

In Gittin ix. 6 and 8 there are rules on the drawing up of the bills of divorce. Both of these sections are concerned with bills of divorce written in both Hebrew and Greek, and not in Aramaic. In Menahoth vi. 3 there are rules about the meal-offering of the Priests. The relevant passage reads: "The cakes required to be mingled [with oil] and the wafers to be anointed. How did they anoint them? In the form of [a cross like the Greek letter] Chi." Greek, therefore, it seems from the evidence of the Mishnah, played its albeit small part in the Temple worship.

Of course the Mishnah is a second-century production. Much of the preparatory work was done in the period up to 130 A.D., when the Bar Cocheba revolt broke out, by a number of scholars including Eliezer ben Hyrcanus, Eliezer ben Jacob, Joshua ben Hananiah and Eleazar ben Azariah, who were among the contemporaries of Rabbi Gamaliel II. The most outstanding figure of this period is, however, Akiba, who was put to death during the Bar Cocheba revolt. After his death his disciples continued his teachings and his method, and furnished the link between Akiba's teaching and the Oral Law as defined in the Mishnah of Rabbi Judah the Patriarch, whom the Talmuds recognize as the editor of this vast work.

As Danby records,[26] the "Rabbi", as he is always styled,

> was born in A.D.135 on the day that Akiba was put to death.... His early life had been spent at the patriarchal court at Usha, in Galilee, where he had as his teacher R. Judah ben Ilai, whose opinions are cited in the Mishnah more frequently than those of any other authority.... We are told that the language always spoken in his home was not the Aramaic dialect then current in Palestine, but Hebrew, the Holy language: even the maid-servants of the household spoke a pure Hebrew. He was also, we learn, an apt student of Greek.

Although this concerns a period over a century later than the time of Jesus, it is still significant evidence for our purpose. Danby points out that the Mishnah records the opinions of the Pharisean party "which were not those of the Sadducean party (whose standards briefly prevailed during the century before the destruction of Jerusalem)."[27] Now the Mishnah indicates that there was no antipathy towards the Greek language in Pharisean circles. It recognizes that Greek is the other acceptable language beside Hebrew for the Scriptures. The Rabbi, who grew up in Galilee, as did Jesus, was "an apt student of Greek". When it is remembered that it was the Sadducees, and not the Pharisees, who were the pro-Hellenistic party, the predominance of the Greek language in Palestine in the time of Jesus is further substantiated.

Furthermore, from the life-style in which the Rabbi was brought up, it is evident that pockets of Hebrew continued to prevail in family situations, and not only in scholarly circles. Anyone who knows anything about bilingualism, or has experience of it, would expect this. The sweeping statements made by New Testament scholars concerning the wide demise of Hebrew and the dominance of Aramaic are not in accord either with the evidence or with what normally happens in bilingual or trilingual situations. It is far more likely that all three languages co-existed in Palestine, as spoken languages during the lifetime of Jesus. Hebrew would, most probably, be spoken by the smallest group, but as the Rabbi's upbringing indicates, it would survive within devout and educated families. Aramaic would occupy an important, but declining position (declining during the previous two centuries) especially in the peasant Jewish home. But the dominant language for almost all communication outside the home would, most probably, be the *lingua franca* of Greek.

Comparatively few opportunities are available for New Testament scholars to live in a bilingual society which bears some resemblance to that of Palestine, and in particular, that of Galilee, in the first century A.D. In Britain, however, there is one area which provides such an opportunity: that is in North and Mid-Wales. There, in a country about the size of Palestine, people speak the indigenous Welsh language, but also speak English, which, like Greek before it, has become the *lingua franca* of so much of the rest of the world. The present writer is a son of a Welsh-speaking mother of "the Dispersion" (she migrated to the Midland counties of England on marriage), and he himself has spent a considerable amount of time in the Welsh-speaking areas of North Wales in the last twenty years. In consequence of this experience it is pertinent to make three points at this stage. The first is that in both spoken and written English, "Welshisms" come through in both the speech and the writing of Welsh people whose "home" language is Welsh. Secondly, the "home" Welsh adopts, and makes its own, many loan-words from English. Danby points out that both the Hebrew of the Mishnah and later Aramaic have a great many Greek loan-words, and even a few Latin ones. This is a feature of bilingualism. Thirdly, it is extremely difficult to tell whether a letter or an article written by a bilingual Welshman in English was first written in Welsh and then translated into English, or written only in English. All these points are of considerable significance in a discussion on the Aramaisms found in the Gospels. In respect of the last point, if it is extremely difficult to adjudicate upon the issue at such a short distance in time, it must be extremely hazardous even for the most erudite of that small band of Aramaic scholars, to claim that a work written in Greek some nineteen centuries ago was first written in Aramaic and then translated into Greek, rather than that it was first written by a bilingual Palestinian Jew, whose home language was Aramaic. (See Appendix B)

This matter of "Welshisms" coming through into English is not only the experience and opinion of the present writer. In the book *The Story of English* which accompanied the impressive B.B.C. television series on this subject, the following is stated:

> The strength of this Welsh culture has permeated the English spoken in Wales. Eluned Phillips, winner of the Eisteddfod Crown, believes that Welsh-English speakers can always be identified by the lilt of their speech. She remarks that even with Richard Burton, who spoke almost perfect Standard English, his Welsh roots were recognizable in "the melodious lilt of his voice and the sing-song way he used to talk English, the resonance, the rounded vowels—in the music of the language."[28]

What is even more important, though, is that Eluned Phillips states that the Welshness of the English spoken in Wales also appears in the sentence construction. She says,

> In Welsh we tend to invert our sentences, perhaps putting the adjective after the noun.... I was talking to a neighbour the other day. She is from the valleys and we were talking about a young Welshman who had died. What she said to me was, "Pity it was that he died so early," which is really a literal translation of the Welsh.[29]

It is quite obvious that the New Testament scholars of the last century, learned men that they were, were completely ignorant of how bilingualism works. If they had paused to consider whether the Aramaic colouring of the Greek of St Mark might have been caused because the writer was bilingual, they might have come to very different conclusions. In fact, they should have suspected that there was bilingualism, or even trilingualism in Palestine because the Gospel of St John declares that Pilate put the title "Jesus of Nazareth, the King of the Jews" in three languages, Hebrew, Greek and Latin. Scholars argue that by "Hebrew" the writer meant Aramaic. This may have been so, but, again, it is conjecture. The author might well have known what he was doing when he wrote "Hebrew", for it might have been in that language that Pilate caused the inscription to be made. Most of the Aramaic-speaking Jews would have been able to read the inscription in Greek, but some of the most devout of the Pharisean sect, who kept alive the Hebrew, might have declined to read such an inscription which was not in Hebrew. This, of course, is conjectural, but it shares that position with the suggesion that the author meant Aramaic when he wrote the word "Hebrew".[30]

There is one aspect of the comparison between the bilingualism of Aramaic-Greek and Welsh-English where the analogy breaks down. In recent years the Welsh language has become a focus of nationalism. This has not always been so. To the present writer's certain knowledge, there was very little nationalistic sentiment associated with the Welsh language in the inter-war years, in the small towns and villages of North Wales. As has been argued above, there is no reason to suppose that Aramaic was a focus of nationalism in first-century Palestine, B.C. or A.D., and there is no evidence to support such a view. If there had been any such nationalist sentiment it would have been asociated with Hebrew. Indeed, the need which some Welsh people have seen for associating the language with nationalistic sentiment was not present in Palestine. The Jews already had a powerful unifying factor in their religion, whereas in Wales the language is the only obvious factor which can be used for such a nationalistic cause.

To return to Aramaic: Meyers and Strange state that it is the great library of Qumran which provides most of the manuscripts composed or translated into Aramaic, indicating that Aramaic was definitely a literary language.

However, they say that the Dead Sea Scrolls are far more often extant in Hebrew than Aramaic, and they explain this fact by suggesting that, in contrast to Palestine in general, the residents of Qumran read and wrote Hebrew. They are much less sure, though, that these people spoke Hebrew. Some scholars suggest that even at Qumran Hebrew was a second language used by scholars, much like Latin in the Middle Ages.

The Aramaic manuscripts from Qumran include the Genesis Apocryphon and the Targum of Job. There are also a number of fragments of other works including the Prayer of Nabonidus, the Testament of the Twelve Patriarchs, the Description of the New Jerusalem, and the Book of Enoch. One of the problems for our purpose, though, is that scholars differ widely in their dating of these manuscripts in Aramaic. Some scholars date them from the third to the first century B.C, whilst others believe some were composed in the first century A.D.

Meyers and Strange prefer to consider the evidence from Qumran in association with other archaeological discoveries from other parts of Palestine. They say it is ossuary inscriptions which provide a greater understanding of Aramaic as a colloquial language. They have discovered significant numbers of these ossuaries, and they clearly indicate the importance and, frequently, the predominance of Aramaic. The closer one gets to the Christian era, however, the more they also indicate the spread and growth of the dominance of Greek.

Reference has already been made to the immense period of time during which Hebrew and Aramaic co-existed in Palestine. It may surprise many, however, that Greek was no "Johnny come lately" upon the Palestinian scene. A. D. Momigliano, contributing to the recently published book *The Legacy of Greece*,[31] states that from the tenth century B.C. Greeks went to Palestine as slaves, merchants and mercenaries. He states that King David apparently employed Cretan mercenaries. Greek pottery has been found at the site of Samaria dating from before the destruction in 722 B.C. In Ashkalon, Greek pottery appears at the end of the seventh century. Momigliano goes on to say:

> When the Jews returned from the Babylonian exile in the fifth century, traffic with the Greeks was re-established. Ashdod, the Philistine capital, has yielded abundant Athenian pottery of the late sixth and fifth centuries. In the fourth century some Greeks lived in Acco, and the earliest coins of Judaea imitate Athenian coins.[32]

Momigliano goes on to point out that in the Old Testament Greece is known as Ionia, and that Cyprus is known as Kittim. There are references to Kittim, son of Javan, in Genesis x. 4, and in Numbers xxiv. 24, which indicates something of the length of time that Cyprus had been known to the writers of the Old Testament. In the Hellenistic age, Kittim became the name for Greeks in general, the Seleucids in particular, and even the Romans.

John Bright[33] and many other scholars affirm the fact that Greek influence affected Palestine long before the conquest of Alexander the Great. Meyers and Strange point out that Greek pottery of the sixth century B.C. has been excavated in various coastal sites, and that Greek coins and the Palestinian imitations are common from the fourth century B.C. They say, "Our earliest dated Greek document... is to be found among the ostraca from Khirbel-el-Kôm."

They refer to the seven ostraca discovered, of which five are in Aramaic, one in Greek, and one in Aramaic and Greek. The date of the bilingual one corresponds with 25 July, 277 B.C.

This dated ostracon, of course, brings us right into the Hellenistic period in Palestine, and what might have been a trickle of Greek influence now becomes a flood. To digress from this for a moment: it is important to recall that by the beginning of the third century B.C. there were more Jews living outside Palestine than there were in the homeland. The vast majority of these adopted Greek as their language, and it was for them that the Septuagint was first written. As Momigliano points out, this was not the only translation of the Scriptures into Greek, for there were at least three other versions, by Aquila, Symmachus and Theodotian, although the Septuagint was always the most famous and most widely used. It is inconceivable that the large numbers of Jews who were Greek-speaking, living in Egypt (a million by the first century A.D.) were cut off from verbal communication with their fellow Jews in Palestine. Martin Noth[34] argues that there was "constant intercourse between the Diaspora and the homeland" in the third century B.C., and that this could not have been effected if some of the homeland Jews, at least, had not been bilingual. Referring to a later period, that is, the first century A.D., Momigliano writes:

> The Palestinian leaders took care to have the approval of the Egyptian Jews.... The Palestinian sages accepted Greek as a language into which the Bible could be translated; at least one sage was convinced that it was the only language. (Mishnah, Megillah i. 8)

In Ptolemaic times, Momigliano claims,

> Greek armies frequently marched through the country. ...Many Jews were taken away as slaves, others became soldiers or military colonists of Hellen-

> istic kings (especially, of course, of the Ptolemies). ... A Greek education became desirable even in Judaea, both for its intrinsic merit and for its usefulness in daily contacts with the rulers. ... The Tobiads were among the first to have Greek tutors. Greek-speaking centres multiplied around the tiny territory of Judaea through colonization and assimilation of the local upper class. The Greek gymnasium began to cast its shadow on the Jewish school (yeshiva) connected with the synagogue.[35]

Furthermore, he says, "Jews very often took or were given Greek names... often a Jew received two personal names, a Hebrew one for use within the community, and a Greek one for external contacts (and possibly domestic life)."[36] Momigliano somewhat laconically comments: "The Greeks were seldom prepared to make any effort to learn a foreign language."[37]

There is, of course, ample evidence of the growth of bilingualism in Palestine. Meyers and Strange give examples of numerous Greek inscriptions found in Palestine from the late third century B.C. to the first century A.D. They also point to the large corpus of Greek literature emanating from Palestine at the same period. Political developments also give indications of the spread of the Greek language, and of Hellenistic influence. John Hyrcanus' sons had Greek names (or nick-names) and in him is seen the irony of the grandson of Mattathias, the initiator of the Maccabean revolt, itself a protest against Hellenization, approaching the pro-Hellenistic Sadducees, who themselves must be evidence for the ever-increasing extension of the Greek language.

In respect of this reaction, which presented many Jews, not only in Judaea, with a real dilemma, Momigliano points out that

> Even the earliest account of the Maccabean revolution,

written in five books by Jason of Cyrene (c. 160 B.C.) and summarized in the extant 2 Maccabees (c. 124 B.C.), is evidence of Hellenization; the tale is told in Greek in the style of popular pathetic historiography.

Momigliano goes on,

> There is no end to the story of the penetration of Greek words, customs, and intellectual habits into Judaea during the rule of the Hasmoneans and the subsequent reign of Herod. The contradictory statements in Talmudic literature about the value and legitimacy of Greek are based on the reality of the power and influence of Greek culture in Palestine. Hermeneutic rules derived from Greek tradition were adopted by rabbis; Greek legal terminology was borrowed; Greek was used in inscriptions on ritual objects of the Temple; a synagogue in Caesarea used Greek in the liturgy. A famous Talmudic passage (Bab. Sotah 49f.) speaks of 500 students of Greek wisdom and 500 of Hebrew wisdom in the school of Gamaliel (A.D. 100) which is a symbolic indication of the penetration of Greek culture into rabbinic schools.[38]

In his recent book *Discovering Jerusalem*, Nahman Avigad writes,

> The coins of Alexander Jannaeus (103–76 B.C.) which we found in large numbers, are inscribed "Of King Alexander" in Greek, and "Jonathan the King" or "Jonathan the High Priest" in archaizing Hebrew. [N.B. not in Aramaic.] Jonathan was Alexander's Hebrew name.... We also uncovered a hoard of twenty-three coins of Mattathias Antigonus, last of the Hasmonaean kings (40–37 B.C.) "Of King Antigonus" in Greek, and "Mattathias, the High Priest and *hever* of the Jews" in archaizing Hebrew.[39]

Josephus points out that even a later high priest is found bearing a Greek name. He says that one of the sons of the high priest Annas (of the Gospels), who was high priest A.D. 37 to 40, bore the name of Theophilus.

Herod the Great was, fundamentally, a Hellenistic-Pagan ruler. Avigad says that Herod

> was among the most extreme admirers of Hellenistic–Roman culture, and his desire to gain a standing for Jerusalem equal to that of the foremost Hellenistic cities led him to imbue his capital with a decidedly Hellenistic flavour. This found expression in the dominant architectural style of the buildings and their monumental proportions, as well as in the current life style, which called for theatres, gymnasium, hippodromes and "the games", a cosmopolitan atmosphere and a luxurious court. This was neither entirely new or unique in Jerusalem where Hellenistic influence had already taken hold among the Jews of the city under the Hasmonaeans.[40]

Avigad also makes the comment that it is generally assumed that the Jerusalem nobility was of the Saducean faction, whilst the lower classes tended more to the Pharisaic faction, which often opposed foreign influences. But this must be just a generalization, as is shown by the fact that Josephus was a Pharisee, but was still able to write in Greek.

Avigad is not, of course, just theorizing. His statements are substantiated by his extensive archaeological discoveries in Jerusalem. He writes,

> In a house which was probably built in the late Hasmonaean period, flourished in the second half of the first century B.C., and was destroyed at the turn of the millennium or very early in the first century A.D., pottery, representing some of the finest produced in late

Hellenistic times, and considered to be manufactured along the eastern littoral of the Mediterranean have been found. Many vessels of this type have been found along with pottery produced in Italy. ...These vessels show that upper-class inhabitants of Jerusalem followed the international flavour of the day.[41]

Storage jars for wine, having Latin "trademarks", were also found, though Avigad wonders how the Gentile wine was used in Jerusalem when the precepts forbidding consumption of foreign products were invoked. He concludes that there have always been more and less observant Jews. He states that his particular house seems to have been deliberately demolished for the construction of a new road.

Avigad also excavated a mansion/palace building in Jerusalem that had fine-quality frescoes, of the kind which were very common in Hellenistic cities in Asia Minor, and which originated in Greece. It is also significant, however, that similar frescoes have been found at the Tel Anafa site in Upper Galilee, which is another indication of how widespread this example of Hellenistic influence was. Avigad says that it appears that these frescoes survived in Palestine when they had become *passé* in the Hellenistic world at large. One Jerusalem fresco depicts fluted Ionic columns bearing a schematic Doric frieze. In the same mansion a stepped pool containing late Hellenistic potsherds, used in Jewish rites of purification, was found. The number of pools discovered seems to indicate that there was virtually a cult of immersion. This mansion, he says, was "clearly a dwelling of a wealthy patrician family of some stature in Jerusalem society. ...The large, magnificent reception hall, and several guest rooms, were all decorated in Hellenistic-Roman fashion."[42] It seems that this mansion was destroyed about A.D. 70.

Avigad gives many more instances of Hellenistic finds during his excavations, not least the interesting "Burnt

House" which was discovered in January 1970. In all there were extensive finds of pottery, stone tables, and inscriptions. He says that in the Hasmonaean period "Greek letters were generally used as numerals in Judaea." In respect of two small bone discs discovered which seem to be related to the theatre, he says, "In our context, the fact that Hellenistic cultural influences did not bypass Jerusalem, even in the realm of pastimes, is significant in itself, regardless of the precise interpretation of the discs."[43]

To return to Herod and his descendants: Avigad gives an interesting quotation from Josephus. He says that when the Temple was completed in the time of Herod Agrippa II, some 18,000 labourers were thrown out of work. Apparently the king agreed to use this redundant labour to pave the streets of Jerusalem in white stone. Josephus notes that "even if a man worked but one hour a day he received wages for the entire day."[44] This seems to echo Jesus' parable of the Labourers in the Vineyard.

Herod the Great's building activity was extensive. He built temples dedicated to pagan gods and to emperor worship, halls and theatres in the Greek style, palaces, castles and baths throughout the land. On the ancient site of Samaria he built a new city, named Sebaste, in honour of the Emperor Augustus. On the coast, on the site of the ancient Straton's Tower, he built a new city and port which he named Caesarea, and which later was to be the capital of the country.

His sons continued this pattern. Philip rebuilt the city of Panias at the source of the Jordan, and named it Caesarea Philippi, where, according to S[t] Matthew, Peter made his famous confession. He raised Bethsaida to the status of a city, and renamed it Julias after the daughter of Augustus; this city/village seems to have been known to Jesus. Philip's brother Antipas showed his disdain for Jewish nationalistic sentiment. Not only did he build his magnificent residence on the Western shore of Lake Gennesaret, and call it

Tiberias, but his first residence, Sepphoris, was an Hellenistic Roman city which lay scarcely four miles North of Jesus' home village of Nazareth. Sepphoris was the largest city in Galilee, and had a fort and a theatre. Also, as Finegan says, "Nazareth was by no means a small out-of-the-way place hidden in a corner of the land, but was on or near important thoroughfares carrying extensive traffic."[45] Meyers and Strange support this view.

By the time of Jesus, this small country, which measured from Caesarea Philippi to Beersheba approximately one hundred and fifty miles, and is nowhere wider than seventy-five miles, was dotted with cities bearing Hellenistic names. Caesarea, Caesarea Philippi, Sepphoris and Bethsaida/Julias have already been mentioned, but there were numerous others including Tiberias, Ptolemais, Scythopolis and Pella (both in the Decapolis), Antipatris, Alexandra and Sebaste, which was near Bethlehem. The great cities of Tyre and Sidon were closely adjacent.

If all this were not sufficient, archaeology provides extensive evidence for the presence of the Greek language, and hence probably bilingualism in Palestine. Josephus states that the sanctuary of the Temple in Jerusalem was separated from the courts of the Gentiles by a barrier three cubits in height. He says that this barrier had thirteen gates, each of which bore an inscription in Latin and Greek threatening death to any Gentile who might seek to enter. An example of this inscription, virtually intact, has been found. Various publications have photographs of this inscription.[46] Now it is true that the readers of the inscriptions were to be Greek-speaking Gentiles, but the composers must have been Greek-speaking Jews of Jerusalem.

Meyers and Strange, speaking of the "House of S[t] Peter" in Capernaum, describe the one hundred and thirty one graffiti scratched on the plaster, in Greek, Aramaic, Latin and Syriac. Even more importantly they state that

> Looking at the known figures concerning ossuary in-

scriptions we find that out of a corpus of 194 inscribed ossuaries, 26% are inscribed in Hebrew or Aramaic, 9% in Greek and a Semitic language, and 64% in Greek alone.[47]

As these two scholars point out, almost two thirds of these inscriptions are in Greek alone. They quote from a number of these inscriptions and conclude that "these prove beyond any reasonable doubt that the majority of Jewish families could read and write Greek, and did so even for strictly family business."[48]

It seems, therefore, careless to say the least for someone like Albrecht Dihle to write, "The Aramaic-speaking population in the countryside was scarcely involved in what went on in the world at large."[49] Meyers and Strange seem much nearer the truth when they state that

> There is every evidence of a close continuum between the Jews of Palestine and the Jews of the Diaspora. A study of the funerary inscriptions from the Beth She arim (truly a Jewish town) that are in Greek has shown that Semitic and Hellenistic views of afterlife are so closely interwoven that the mere dominance of the Greek language is not sufficient to indicate the degree of accommodation to Hellenism.[50]

The Wisdom of Solomon is significant in this respect; and whilst most modern commentators would describe this as the work of an Alexandrian Jew, it is worthwhile remembering that R.H.Charles, in his classification, included this book in his didactic section of Palestinian Jewish literature.

Albrecht Dihle's view would contradict what Meyers and Strange say in the above quotation. Dihle writes, "The impact of Jesus can be understood historically only against the background of his country's Judaism, which on the surface had become part of the Graeco-Roman world, but at bottom was completely estranged from it."[51] This is, in fact, an hypothesis; a very commonly held hypothesis it is true, upon which great theological edifices have been built, but which flies in the face of the evidence. Subconsciously, Dihle seems to recognize this, for he continues, "We know, however, of this impact only from sources written in Greek, which at every turn betray Hellenistic concepts in varying degrees."[52]

In view of this undeniable fact, the dogmatism of the first statement quoted from Dihle is quite remarkable. What Dihle seems to be saying is, "The evidence suggests X, but my hypothesis requires Y, therefore X must be jettisoned." To claim, as Dihle does, that the Aramaic-speaking population in the countryside was scarcely involved in what went on in the world at large reveals a naïveté which is scarcely credible. The long arm of the tax collector, collecting taxes on behalf of the Roman occupier, would not ignore and leave alone the Aramaic-speaking population, and when people pay heavy taxes it is rarely indeed that they do not concern themselves with what is going on in the rest of the country. Dihle's imaginative picture of the Aramaic-speaking population is one which suggests a ghetto-like isolation in some areas, and is another excursus into historical fiction. The geography of Palestine, with, as has been indicated above, the wide distribution of Hellenistic towns throughout the country, indicates how false a picture Dihle seeks to provide. Furthermore, especially in the procuratorship of Pontius Pilate, it is extremely unlikely that any Jew would ignore, and remain unconcerned with, what was going on. The carrying of standards into Jerusalem bearing the likeness of the emperor which so violated Jewish principles and provoked determined and successful protest; the taking of money from the Temple treasury to build an aqueduct in Jerusalem; the incident recorded in Luke xiii. 1, of the mingling of the blood of certain Galileans with their sacrifices (which certainly had not escaped Jesus' ears, nor, apparently, theirs who listened to him) and the slaughter of a multitude of Samaritans who had gathered at Mount Gerizim to search for sacred vessels—all ordered by Pilate—would scarcely leave even the most countrified Jew unmoved. It is plain that here again we have another New Testament scholar who is working in the genre of historical fiction. What is more, like others of his contemporaries, Dihle is so inconsistent in his historical fiction! He is very anxious to insist on the "Jewishness" of the population in the countryside, yet he believes that they would be unconcerned with all those acts which challenge and threaten their Jewishness.

Günther Bornekamm makes a similar excursus. He writes:

> Jesus' mother tongue is the Aramaic of Galilee...we do not know to what extent he and his disciples knew Greek, widely used in administration and commerce. At any rate we find in Jesus no trace of the influence of Greek philosophy or of the Greek manner of livng, just as nothing is known of activity on his part in the Hellenistic towns of the country. Rather we hear of his activity in the smaller hamlets and villages—Bethsaida, Chorazin, Capernaum, in the hill country and round the sea of Galilee.[53]

Bornekamm apparently did not know that Philip had raised Bethsaida to the status of a city and renamed it Julias, or that Capernaum was hardly a purely Jewish town. As Léon Dufour said, "Jesus went to live in Capernaum...in order that the light might arise in Gentile-occupied Galilee." (Cf. Matthew iv. 14–16)[54] Bornekamm also appears to have quite overlooked Mark vii. 31, which expressly states that Jesus went into the Decapolis, after being in the regions of Tyre and Sidon. Bornekamm also appears to forget (though it is difficult to see how anyone with even a nodding acquaintance with the Gospels could so forget) the episode which Matthew records as happening at Caesarea Philippi, which has had such far-reaching implications for the history of Christendom, and for the relationship between the Roman Catholic Church and all other Churches. Some scholars, in addition, have sought to suggest that Jesus went only to the "regions" of Tyre and Sidon, and studiously avoided the cities themselves. This, however, is a quite gratuitous assumption for which there is no evidence whatsoever. Jesus may or may not have entered the cities themselves. Beyond that the evidence provides no clues. Such a conjecture shares with Bornekamm and Dihle a concern with the genre of historical fiction.

CHAPTER IV

The Gospels and the Aramaic Hypothesis

No Aramaic document of the early Christian Church has ever been discovered. If scholars were to discover another ancient religion which had arisen in a country where two languages "A" and "B", or even three languages "A", "B" and "C", were to some extent spoken, and all the early literature of that religion was in language "A", the onus to demonstrate that the founder and first members of that religion spoke and taught not in "A" but in "B" or "C" would be on those who sought to propound such a theory. In respect of primitive Christianity, however, the opposite has been the case. The only evidence that any early Christian writing in Aramaic ever existed, as far as the present writer can discover, is in the statement of Papias, cited by Eusebius: "Matthew compiled the Sayings in the Aramaic language and every one translated them as well as he was able." The first question which arises is: did Papias mean Aramaic, or did he write and mean Hebrew? J. Stevenson and most other translators of Eusebius translate the word as "Hebrew",[55] whilst most theologians imply that Papias is referring to Aramaic. Other questions also arise. What did Papias mean by "Sayings"? Historians seem to believe that he meant the Gospel, whilst theologians think he did not. Charles Bigg wrote,

When Papias says that Matthew composed the Oracles in Hebrew he means that he was in the fullest sense the author of the First Gospel, and he wrote it in his native tongue. Neither statement would now be admitted.[56]

Bigg is supported by B. J. Kidd. On the other hand T. W. Manson writes, "A collection of oracles is a singularly inept description of the Gospel."[57] Further he says,

> The argument of Donovan (*The Logia in Ancient and Recent Literature*, 1924) that the Greek *ta logia*, "the oracles", must in this context mean the canonical Gospel of Matthew, rests on a series of mis-interpretations of the term as used in the Septuagint, New Testament, and contemporary Jewish and early Christian writings.[58]

The attitude of scholars towards Papias is ambivalent, and the conflict is between New Testament theologians and Church historians. It does not occur to Manson that Papias might be a person who would make "a singularly inept description of the Gospel". It cannot be known whether Papias was describing something other than the Gospel, or whether he made an unfortunate choice of word. New Testament theologians are apt to choose the interpretation which fits their hypothesis. For instance, referring to Papias' statement that Mark was the interpreter of Peter, Vincent Taylor comments: "I hope I have given adequate ground to the invaluable Papias tradition, which is so sound that, if we did not possess it, we should be compelled to postulate something very much like it." This comment shows the readiness of New Testament scholars to postulate hypothetical evidence, when real evidence is unavailable. In contrast to Taylor, other scholars are ready to quote Eusebius' sardonic comment on Papias: "He was evidently a man of exceedingly small intelligence, as one might judge from his discourses." F. J. Foakes Jackson wrote,

> Papias seems to have had a great capacity of acquiring information combined with almost unlimited credulity. ... Irenaeus quotes a passage about the abundant plenty which the elect will enjoy in the time of the millennium, which helps to mitigate our regret that so large a portion of his writings is lost.[59]

Further, whilst T. W. Manson decides, "We may therefore conclude that the statement of Papias is material he derived from an earlier generation,"[60] B. J. Kidd concludes that "The truth appears to be that neither Papias nor his informants knew much more of the process by which the Synoptic Gospels took shape than may be gathered from their contents. In that case they must have assumed their present shape earlier than is commonly supposed."[61] It is evident, therefore, that Papias' evidence for the existence of an Aramaic original of the Gospel according to S[t] Matthew is not without its problems.

In his book from which the above quotations are taken, T. W. Manson reveals how conjecture can be preferred to evidence. He writes:

> The question now arises: granting that Jesus did teach, was He a teacher in the proper Jewish sense? Was He, so to speak, academically qualified for the title of Rabbi? Popular fancy has generally preferred to think of the simple carpenter of Nazareth, who, by His superior insight confounds the learned. But such information as we have points rather in the opposite direction. The fact that He was addressed by his opponents as "Teacher" is difficult to explain unless He was in fact recognised by them as their equal in point of scholarship. The quotations from the Old Testament in His teaching show a close familiarity with the five books of the Law, most of the prophetic books, and Psalms, Job and Daniel in the third division of the Hebrew canon. It is probable that He knew the Old Testament in Hebrew, and, I think,

possible at least that He was acquainted with the Rabbinic Hebrew used in the schools of the Law. If Jesus used this language at all, it would be in His dealings with the learned. The impression left by the accounts of His controversies with these men is not that they saw in Him a village craftsman turned amateur theologian but rather a competent scholar who had developed heretical tendencies.[62]

Here is an outstanding example of hypothesis building, of placing untested and untestable conjectures one upon another. In his great book *The Quest of the Historical Jesus*, Schweitzer pointed out the strong tendency of theologians to fall into the trap of portraying Jesus in terms of their own contemporaries. Manson has truly fallen into this trap.

Manson asks, "Was Jesus academically qualified for the title of Rabbi?" This question is entirely anachronistic. It is quite mistaken to suggest that first-century Judaism had a system similar to that of modern European universities, where a student has to be "academically qualified" before he can assume the title of "doctor". Similarly anachronistic are the ideas of "amateur theologian" and "competent scholar who had developed heretical tendencies". Such terms are totally out of place in respect of first-century Judaism. Even more serious, however, is the fact that Manson has to ignore New Testament evidence to propound his theory. It is not popular fancy which portrays Jesus as the carpenter of Nazareth, but the Gospels. Manson ignores Mark vi. 3 ff., and its parallel in Matthew xiii. 55–8. Whether Jesus was "the carpenter" as in the Markan version, or "the son of the carpenter" as in the Matthean version, the important questions are "Where did this man get all this? What wisdom is given to him? What mighty works are wrought by his hands? Is not this the carpenter, the son of Mary, and brother of James and Joses and Judas and Simon, and are not his sisters here with us?" If Jesus was an academically qualified rabbi who had gone heretical, his contemporaries at Nazareth knew nothing of it. Such comments upon Jesus, "the simple carpenter of Nazareth", however, are not confined to the synoptic Gospels. In the Gospel according to St John, vii. 15, it states, "The Jews marvelled at it saying 'How is it that this man has learning, when he has never studied?'"

It is also difficult to see what Manson achieves by his listing of certain parts of the Old Testament, claiming Jesus' acquaintance with them. His two mentions of Hebrew seem little more than an attempt to buttress a weak argument, especially when it is realized that the vast majority of Jesus' quotations from the Old Testament, as given in the New, are not made from the Hebrew version but from the Septuagint. This matter is demonstrated in a later chapter. In fact, Manson gives no evidence for his conjecture that Jesus "was acquainted with the Rabbinic Hebrew used in the schools of the Law."

Furthermore, there seems to be a strange schizophrenia which appears to assail New Testament scholars from time to time. This can be seen in Manson's writings. Virtually every saying of Jesus can be rejected as not truly his *ipsissima verba*, but when it suits the purpose of an hypothesis a particular saying can be taken as being from a first-hand eye-witness reporter. The fact of the matter is that it is not known with anything like certainty under what circumstances a man might be called "rabbi". Manson, for example, completely ignores the fact that in first-century-A.D. Palestine, according to St Matthew (xxiii. 8), Jesus expressly rejects the title or description of Rabbi, and the only other use of "rabbi" for Jesus in that Gospel is found on the lips of Judas. The Gospel according to St Luke does not use the word "rabbi" at all. In Mark the usages to which Manson refers are as follows: twice by Peter (ix. 5 and xi. 21), once by Judas (xiv. 45), and once by the Blind Bartimaeus (x. 51) where the term recorded is, in the Nestlé text,

The Gospels and the Aramaic Hypothesis

Rabboni. There is, however, some degree of textual variation here, and the R.S.V. prefers to translate by using the word "master". It is little less than astonishing that an eminent New Testament scholar should have built up a substantial hypothesis upon such a small and fragile base.

If the qualifications necessary for the title "rabbi" in New Testament times are obscure, those required for the use of the titles "master" or "teacher", used in all four Gospels, are even more so. It could be, and there is a good deal of evidence to suggest this, that anyone who gathered around himself a group of followers, or disciples, and taught, privately to these disciples and/or also to the public at large, could be called "teacher" or "master", just as in present-day America anyone who exercises the office of minister of religion, whether he be trained or not trained, is called "reverend" or, quite frequently, "pastor". In contradistinction to Manson's claim, the fact that Jesus was addressed by his opponents as "Teacher" is not "difficult to explain". In his most penetrating and revealing book *Jesus's Audience*, J. Duncan M. Derrett points out how immensely important prestige was in the society and culture in which Jesus was born and grew up. It was, no doubt, a common and widely accepted courtesy to call anyone who was engaged in public teaching, "Teacher". It is not improbable that whilst Jesus' enemies followed the common courtesy and referred to him as "Teacher", a sardonic tone was not absent from this description.

Further, in respect of this matter, Derrett argues that "There was no organised education in Palestine," and, significantly, he goes on to point out that there was a class of teachers who were also healers. Jesus would certainly have fitted into this category. It is very likely that a teacher who also possessed some charismatic appearance and attraction provided an added dimension to the situation. The kind of society in which Jesus grew up and lived was far more likely to give both credence and respect to a charismatic teacher, than to be concerned with some kind of academic qualifications. There can be little doubt that Jesus was a man with a powerful charisma.

Manson also speaks, in the quotation above, of the possibility of Jesus speaking Hebrew. The fact of the matter is that it is not known whether or not Jesus spoke Hebrew, because there is no evidence available. If his home at Nazareth was like that of the Rabbi Judah the Patriarch (see p. 39, above) it could be that in his devout household nothing but pure Hebrew was spoken. Of course, that might imply other similarities with the Rabbi; for example, that Aramaic was not spoken, and that Jesus was an apt student of Greek, a parallel which would not suit Manson at all. It is evident that Jesus was a highly intelligent man, and he might well have learnt Hebrew, whatever the circumstances of his home.

Manson continues, "It may be taken as certain that the bulk of the teaching [of Jesus] was spoken in Aramaic, the vernacular language of Palestine, and the *only language* [my italics] in which the majority of the people were at home."[63] Now, as has been demonstrated above, and supported by the archaeological finds of both Meyers and Strange, and Avigad, this claim that Aramaic was the only language in which the majority of the people of Palestine were at home is just not true. To quote Meyers and Strange again:

> The cities, or toparchies, of Lower Galilee are all tied into the important trade routes that connect the Sea of Galilee with the coastal plain. [Then follows a description of these routes.] All these lower Galilean sites are thus urbane centres linked to the more pagan and hence Greek-speaking West with its cosmopolitan atmosphere and multilingual population. Topography also enables us to locate the bulk of Jesus' career in Lower Galilee and the Rift Valley region, with headquarters in Capernaum. The isolation often associated with the Gal-

ilean personality is therefore quite inappropriate when we speak of Jesus of Nazareth, who grew up along one of the branches of one of the busiest trade routes in Ancient Palestine.[64]

Manson continues:

> [Aramaic] was their mother tongue as it was the mother tongue of Jesus, the language of His prayers—as is shown by His use of the word *Abba*—and the language which Jesus used in speaking to ordinary folk—as we learn from the stories of Jairus's daughter and the healing of the deaf mute.

In much recent theological writing the little word *Abba* has had to bear an enormous weight, imposed, especially, by New Testament scholars. Many have said, as does J. A. T. Robinson in *Honest to God*, that it was a kind of pet-name for the Father. It is not inappropriate here to consider what James Barr has said about the practice of isolating one word and building great edifices upon it. He writes,

> It is the sentence (and of course the still larger literary complex such as the complete speech or poem) which is the linguistic bearer of the usual theological statement, and not the word (the lexical unit) or the morphological and syntactical connection. ... The point we have here made, namely that the real communication of religious and theological patterns is by the larger word-combinations and not by the lexical units or words, is of real importance for one of the problems which I have mentioned in the beginning, namely the problem of the translation of the Bible—something that is, naturally, of the greatest practical importance for the Church.[65]

No doubt Professor Barr would say the same about the isolation of one word even if it be an Aramaic word, for to wrest such a word out of its context is, as Barr points out, both illicit and the cause of inaccuracies.

In conjunction with Professor Barr's comments it is worth noting that this word *Abba* is used in the Mishnah as a title for certain rabbis, and in this usage there is no hint of an affectionate "pet-name". Furthermore, if what Manson claims is true, that Jesus used Aramaic when speaking to "ordinary folk", and if the Gospels recount this practice, then the conclusion must be that Jesus spoke to remarkably few "ordinary folk". Indeed, and on the contrary, when considered in terms of bilingualism, Jesus' use of Aramaic as described in the Gospels is remarkably logical and consistent. A discussion of these occasions will be found on pp. 74 ff., below.

It would not be easy to find a more typical case of untested hypotheses being built upon other untested hypotheses than this exercise of Manson when he is writing about *The Mission and Message of Jesus*. As has already been pointed out, he begins with the assumption that Jesus taught virtually exclusively in Aramaic. He continues with the untested and in fact false hypothesis that the people of Galilee would really only understand Aramaic. His next hypothesis based upon the two previous ones is that the earliest accounts of Jesus, produced by the Church after the resurrection, were in Aramaic, accounts which no one apart from the possible informant of Papias ever claimed to have seen. He is then faced, however, with the problem that these accounts exist and, as far as can be demonstrated, exist only, in Greek. He also has the problem that if Matthew and Luke had before them a document or series of oracles such as scholars have postulated as "Q", which would be necessarily concerned with Manson's own subject in this book, *The Sayings of Jesus*, it was a document or tradition that was certainly in Greek. Consequently, not only has there to be an hypothetical pre-Greek Aramaic Gospel, but also an hypothetical Aramaic "Q". The permutations of these hypotheses become quite bemusing.

Manson goes on to write,

But Christianity is a missionary religion, and it was not long before the new faith began to spread beyond the borders of Palestine. It may be *conjectured* [my italics] that it was at Antioch (Acts xi. 19ff.) where the Gentiles began to come into the Church in considerable numbers, that the need for a Greek version of the teaching became pressing.[66]

Once again Manson appears to overlook the evidence which would demonstrate the weakness of his conjectures. He fails to realize that it would not be only the Gentiles who would not understand an Aramaic message. Neither would the Hellenistic Jews, and the problems would arise long before the Gospel reached Antioch. It seems reasonable to assume that most Hellenistic Jews would not be Aramaic-speaking. The only alternative would be another conjecture, that the vast majority of the Jews of the Dispersion for some inexplicable reason all learnt Aramaic when they came to Palestine, in spite of the evident fact that their native language, Greek, was widely spoken there. Manson completely ignores Acts vi, which expressly states that in the infant Church there were both Hebrews (Palestinian Jews?) and Hellenists (Jews of the Dispersion). Not only this, but the Seven who were appointed to help solve the problems raised by the Hellenist widows all have Greek names. Although this strongly suggests that all were Hellenists, this is not necessarily so for, as has been mentioned above, many Palestine Jews had Greek names. In passing: if Aramaic was such a dominant and exclusive language in Palestine at the time contemporary with Jesus, it is difficult to see how those who only understood Greek ever heard of the Gospel from the allegedly monoglotic Aramaic-speaking disciples. It is certainly not easy to see in that case how the Palestinian Jewish Christians knew the Hellenists were murmuring, or what they were murmuring about.

Whatever the home lands of the Seven were, the Acts of

the Apostles says quite explicitly that one of the seven was Nicolaus, a proselyte of Antioch, who would be just the kind of person for whom Manson believed that the Greek accounts of the Gospel were written. But how did Nicolaus first come to hear the Gospel if someone did not tell of it to him in Greek? The only solution to such a problem would be another conjecture: that he first learnt Aramaic. Furthermore, whatever the synagogue of "the Freedmen" (which included Cyrenians, Alexandrians and those from Cilicia and Asia) was, if the names mean anything at all it must have been one which was predominantly Hellenistic in membership. Must the hypothesis be created that all these people first learned Aramaic, and that they listened to Stephen's long speech in Aramaic, which, apparently, he must have learnt first in order that he might hear and understand the Gospel? One thing becomes apparent, and that is that for the Aramaic hypothesis to retain any consistency, more and more bizarre conjectures have to be made.

It is in fact the Gospels themselves which provide examples of Jesus speaking Greek, once the probability of bilingualism is accepted. For instance, C. J. Mullo-Weir voices the generally accepted scholarly opinion that "Hebrew had become unintelligible to the common people by the beginning of the Christian era."[67] In spite of this, Mullo-Weir's colleague in the same collection of essays could still argue that the words *iota hen e mia keraia* in Matthew v. 18 are a translation of the Hebrew words Jesus is supposed to have used, although the Greek word *keraia* makes better sense, in this context, than would its Hebrew translation and although according to Mullo-Weir's own statement no one would understand Jesus when he said this in Hebrew anyway.

Again, commentators are concerned to stress that when Jesus went across the Sea of Galilee into the country of the Gerasenes (Mark v. 1 ff.), wherever the precise location of this area might be, he went into Gentile territory. The presence of the pigs indicates this, and it is confirmed by the statement that the restored madman went on to the Decapolis to proclaim what Jesus had done for him. Now if Jesus was not bilingual, the man must have been. The choice for bilingualism has to be between a madman, who might well have been a Gentile and who, apparently, had lived in the Decapolis, and a brilliant, intelligent and articulate teacher. It is difficult to see why the madman, living evidently in a Greek-speaking area, should have learnt Aramaic. It is easy to see why Jesus, living in a bilingual area, should know and speak Greek. In spite of this, the Aramaic hypothesis must insist that it was the madman who was bilingual and Jesus who was monoglotic.

Again, when Jesus went into the region of Tyre (unquestionably a Greek-speaking area), he was accosted, according to Mark, by a Greek/Gentile woman, asking him to heal her daughter. On the basis of the Aramaic hypothesis it has to be assumed that this poor distracted woman could speak Aramaic well enough to understand a quip Jesus made, in spite of the fact that there was no need for her to learn Aramaic, living in a Greek-speaking area. In Greek the word that Jesus used for *the dogs* is a diminutive, suggesting, C. E. B. Cranfield says, that the reference is to the little dogs which were kept as pets. In spite of the fact that in Hebrew and Aramaic there is no corresponding diminutive, commentators cannot allow Jesus to have used this word, but insist that this is the Evangelist's attempt to soften the offensiveness of Jesus' words. Behind this insistence there seems to be almost a kind of distorted docetism, which seeks to protect Jesus from plain speaking. It is difficult to see why Jesus, having been brought up in a bilingual area, would not use the word *kunarion* to an anxious Greek-speaking mother.

Of the place where Jesus was brought up, Meyers and Strange say,

Jesus grew up along one of the branches of one of the busiest trade routes in ancient Palestine, the Way of the Sea (Via Maris). This minor branch became prominent as the significance of nearby Sepphoris grew when in Roman times it became one of the most important administrative centres of the Roman provincial government. Furthermore, Nazareth occupied a commanding position overlooking the Via Maris itself through the Jezreel Valley.[68]

Jesus would have been well acquainted with people like the Gentile woman, and would know in what language to speak to them.

The Aramaic hypothesis would also seek to compel us to believe that the centurion of Matthew viii. 5 ff. (a Greek-speaking officer posted to a bilingual area) from Capernaum (see Léon Dufour's comment on this town quoted above on page 51) had laboriously learnt Aramaic. It is true that he was himself most interested in Judaism, but this interest would by no means compel him to learn Aramaic. There were millions of devout Jews who knew no Aramaic, and many of these journeyed to Jerusalem for the feasts. It does not help the Aramaic case if the Lukan version is preferred to the Matthean, for the centurion would still have to speak to the Jews to ask them to intercede with Jesus on his behalf.

Furthermore, the Aramaic hypothesis would insist that Pontius Pilate "who had scant regard for the scruples of the Jerusalem religious community"[69] set himself the task of learning Aramaic, in spite of the fact that it is as certain as anything can be at this distance in time that the Jewish leaders in Jerusalem, with whom he would need to communicate, spoke Greek. When the atrocities committed by Pilate, and mentioned above (page 53) are taken into consideration, the likelihood of Pilate's choosing to learn Aramaic is about as remote as anything can be. The only alternative to believing that Jesus spoke Greek is to postulate that either there was an interpreter present when Pilate tried Jesus, or that these conversations are nothing more than figments of the imaginations of the four Evangelists who wrote them. Of course, there could be all kinds of bizarre conjectures to support the Aramaic view, such as that Jesus' subsequent silence before Pilate was because he did not understand the language Pilate spoke, or that the crowd, in which there must have been a great many Jews who only spoke Greek, did not understand the Aramaic which Pilate spoke, and that the cry "Crucify" was in response to the promptings (in Greek?) by the High Priests.

There is still more explicit evidence in the Gospels themselves, once the Aramaic blinkers are removed. In John vii. 35 it is reported that the Jews asked "Where does this man [Jesus] intend to go that we shall not find him? Does he intend to go to the Dispersion among the Greeks and teach the Greeks?" Those who maintain the Aramaic hypothesis must declare either that John was mistaken about Jesus—and if they wish to make this assertion they should supply the evidence upon which they are basing it—or they must create a new hypothesis that Jesus intended to go to some first-century language laboratory in order to learn Greek. In respect of these New Testament critics one is faced with the uncomfortable choice of deciding either that they are frequently unobservant of the writings they are supposed to be investigating, or that they are so arrogant that they assume they know the situation in which Jesus lived better, at a range of 2,000 years, than someone who wrote, at the very outside, within a century of Jesus' life. Indeed, one is compelled to wonder whether New Testament scholars ever actually *read* the New Testament apart from dissecting it.

The names of Jesus' disciples provide some interesting insights, and present us with more evidence. Two of the disciples, Andrew and Philip, have quite explicitly Greek names. Of Philip, who came from Bethsaida/Julias, St John says, (xii. 21): "Now among those who went up to worship at the feast were some Greeks. So these came to Philip who was from Bethsaida in Galilee and said to him, 'Sir, we would see Jesus.'" It is difficult to see how anyone could construe the implications of this episode as anything but an acceptance that Philip spoke Greek, though no doubt the ingenuity of critical New Testament scholars and their ability to produce a conjecture which avoids the obvious must not be disregarded. Another disciple on the Markan list has, if not a Greek name, a Graecized form of his name. Thaddaeus may be an hypocristic noun, which describes a person by comparison with something of like nature, and his name may come from the Aramaic word for *breast*, but this is still conjectural. Another disciple apparently had a father with a Greek name: James the son of Alphaeus. Both Alphaeus and Cleopas may be two different forms of the Aramaic Chalpai but, says Plummer,[70] this is uncertain. About Cleopas Lightfoot said, "A man whose real Aramaic name was Clopas might Graecize the word and call himself Cleopas," but for a man so to do would be further evidence of the dominance of Greek and the Greek culture.

There is also the intriguing case of the name Peter. Only in the Fourth Gospel, and then only once, and in 1 Corinthians and Galatians, is the Aramaic form of this name transliterated into Cephas. If Mark, for instance, was using an Aramaic original, as is so often claimed, why did he not use Cephas, insteady of the totally Greek *petros*? The use of the name Peter in the Gospels is very interesting. After the confession at Caesarea Philippi, Matthew never uses the name Simon again. Mark has a similar pattern except that in the garden of Gethsemane Jesus addresses Peter as Simon. This is interesting because this is the only time in the Synoptic Gospels when Jesus addresses Peter *by name* in direct speech. Similarly in John xxi. 15, where again Jesus' words are reported in direct speech, Jesus addresses Peter as "Simon". As will be indicated later, when the incident of

Jairus's daughter is discussed, this is precisely the situation where Jesus would use an Aramaic word rather than a Greek one.

In the Gospel according to St Luke, the name Simon is never used after the calling of the Twelve and, rather curiously, in the Acts of the Apostles, the name Simon is only used in the Cornelius story (x. 5–xi. 13). There is another exception in Acts xv, where James refers to Peter as *Simeon*, rather than Simon. This usage by James may be a link with Paul's usage. Paul only writes about Peter in 1 Corinthians and in Galatians. In Galatians the Nestlé text uses *Cephas* on four occasions (i. 18, ii. 9, 11 and 14). Of these four instances, none is without some textual ambiguity. Some ancient manuscripts substitute the name "Peter" in each case except ii. 9, where the name is omitted. In Chapter Two, Paul also uses the name "Peter", and in these two instances (verses 7 and 8) there are no textual problems. Duncan may well be right when he says,

> Paul introduces the names of the three chief leaders of the Jerusalem church, "James, Cephas and John"; in calling them "pillars", an appropriate designation in connection with the Church as the Temple of God, he is probably using a dignified title applied to them by the Judaizers.[71]

It may be that there is a sardonic element in this Pauline use of Peter's Aramaic name, for there is little doubt that Paul felt that Peter, after initiating the Gentile mission, had let him down very badly. In 1 Corinthians Paul uses the name *Cephas* four times, and does not use the name Peter. Apart from 1 Corinthians xv. 5, all these instances are in the context of controversy. It is possible to speculate as to whether there was any other reason why Paul generally seems to prefer the name Cephas to Peter (never Simon), but this would only be conjecture. It may be observed that amongst bilingual Welshmen, when returning home from a lengthy period of absence in a non-Welsh-speaking environment, even if the rest of their Welsh has become rusty, they will still tend to use Welsh names for their relatives and friends, referring, for instance, to a David as "Dafydd" or "Dewi".

C. K. Barrett is much concerned with John's "mistake", when the evangelist describes Bethsaida as being in Galilee and not Gaulanitis. He thinks John is following "later usage".[72] It could be argued, and there is some evidence, that John was quite correct, and was quoting a much older and more Israelistic tradition, because the whole area was considered to be Galilee for centuries before it was divided politically into such areas as Gaulanitis and Trachonitis. If this is a mistake on John's part it is one he shares with Josephus, who divides the whole area into Upper and Lower Galilee. Whatever might have been the case with regard to John, Josephus certainly knew the area from first-hand experience. He led the Jewish forces in Lower Galilee in the campaigns against Vespasian and Titus, and therefore his evidence should not be dismissed lightly in the face of twentieth-century conjecture. Recent scholarship suggests that, if anything, Upper Galilee was less influenced by Hellenistic customs and language than was Lower Galilee, and this evidence can only weaken the Aramaic hypothesis rather than strengthening it.

Barrett is also at some pains to diminish the significance of the Greek names of Philip and Andrew, saying that in the former case it cannot be held to prove Greek ancestry and in the latter case that it cannot prove Greek connections of the family because this name appears in the Talmud.[73] It is not easy to see why anyone should wish to prove either of these two points. What these names do demonstrate, though, as does Barrett's reference to the Talmud, is the depth of penetration of the Greek language into Jewish family life.

Recent New Testament scholarship seems once more to be linking the Gospel according to S⁺ John with either John the Apostle or another who stood within the Apostolic circle (J. A. T. Robinson, C. H. Dodd, A. M. Hunter, C. F. D. Moule and Léon Dufour). Robinson says, "The Gospel is written in correct but simple Greek, with what might be called an Aramaic accent."[74] The evidence suggests that here is an Apostle, or an apostolic man, close to Jesus, who both spoke and wrote Greek fluently. Also, the majority of commentators identify the author of the Gospel according to S[t] Mark with the John Mark of the Acts of the Apostles; a Jew of Jerusalem, early associated with the Apostles and the apostolic community, who spoke and wrote Greek. Even if he were not John Mark, the Aramaic theorists' own studies imply that here was a Palestinian Jew, who was a close companion of S[t] Peter (cf. Vincent Taylor, quoted above), who spoke and wrote Greek. On the other hand, even if John Mark did not write the second Gospel, there can be little doubt, if words retain any meaning at all, that he was brought up in Jerusalem; hence a Jew of Jerusalem. Again, there can be little doubt that, unless the Acts of the Apostles is a work of complete fiction, when John Mark travelled with Barnabas and Paul on their first missionary journey, a journey which took them into the heart of the Greek-speaking world, he would have had to speak Greek. Here, then, is a Greek-speaking Jew of Jerusalem, who himself provides further evidence of bilingualism in the early Church. Of course, it could be conjectured that Mark spoke only Aramaic, and was entirely dependent upon Barnabas and Paul and their ability to translate for him. It is difficult, however, to see why Barnabas and Paul would wish to take with them such a handicapped companion. It seems that Paul, having studied under Gamaliel in Jerusalem, knew Hebrew and, most likely, some Aramaic too, in addition to the Greek of his native city of Tarsus. Concerning Barnabas, we just do not know what languages he had at his disposal. As a Cypriot he would grow up in a Greek-speaking culture (Acts iv. 36). Whether the fact that he owned property, presumably in the region of Jerusalem but not necessarily so, might imply that he was bilingual, it is just not possible to judge. One thing, however, is certain, and that is, if Mark relied on Barnabas and Paul to translate for him during the mission, when he eventually decided to leave it he would have faced acute difficulties in getting home from Pamphylia speaking only Aramaic.

It is now appropriate to consider in some detail the question of the Aramaic words, and the translations given with them, in the Gospels themselves. When these words are examined and the contexts analyzed, some very interesting points arise. Perhaps the chief one is that in the context of the hypothesis of bilingualism, their use in the Gospels reveals a remarkably consistent pattern, which is in sharp contrast to the reasons that have hitherto been suggested by New Testament scholars.

For instance, concerning the words *Talitha cumi* in the account of the raising of Jairus's daughter (Mark v.41) commentators have claimed that the use of foreign words was a feature of miracle stories. This argument, however, fails on two grounds. First, if this was so, it is remarkable that so few of the stories of Jesus' healing miracles contain these "foreign" words. The only occasion other than the raising of Jairus's daughter is the healing of the deaf mute in Mark vii. 34. The second and much more devastating ground is that these words were not foreign words but Aramaic, in which the same commentators claim that all Jesus' teaching was given. (There is some doubt as to whether *ephphatha* is Aramaic, but see the discussion in Appendix D.) This is yet another example of scholarly conjecture which leads straight into historical fiction.

In respect of these words spoken in Jairus's home some significant questions need to be asked. Why did the evangelist single out the words to the dead child to be expressed in Aramaic? Why were not the words spoken to the woman healed of the haemorrhage also in Aramaic? The evangelist makes it quite clear that these two miracles were performed on the same day, in a similar part of the country; indeed the healing of the woman interrupts the errand of mercy to Jairus's house. It is no answer to be told that the tradition received by Mark did not contain any other Aramaic words, for in response to this further conjecture we would have to ask, "Why did it not?" Such an hypothesis merely shifts the responsibility for the incorporation of the Aramaic words back one stage, and the problem still remains.

In fact the proponents of the Aramaic hypothesis can advance no reasonable explanation for the inclusion of these isolated Aramaic words. In terms of bilingualism, however, there is no problem, and their inclusion makes complete sense. Aramaic, in the Palestine of Jesus' day, was the language of the home, and nothing would be more natural than for Jesus to address the child in the language of her home, rather than in the language of the market place. In fact, this reveals the almost incredible attention to detail by the evangelist, indicating, once more, that the Gospel accounts are most probably a good deal more accurate and reliable than contemporary New Testament critics will allow. To substantiate this claim, it can be observed that a bilingual Welshman will speak English in the English-speaking market place, but will revert to Welsh immediately he crosses his own threshold. A bilingual Welsh doctor visiting a sick child in a Welsh home would invariably speak to the child in Welsh, in spite of the fact that in a great deal of his practice he would speak English. The same pattern of behaviour would be true in German and Spanish bilingual communities in the U.S.A.

With regard to the word *Abba* the situation is not quite so clear. It may be that, as Robinson claims, this word can be used as a kind of "pet name", or, perhaps better expressed, a term of affection or endearment. If the word was used in this way it would be another instance entirely consistent with the practice of bilingualism. A Welsh-speaking woman living in England will still use Welsh words of affection to her children such as "bach" and "cariad", in spite of the otherwise totally English context. This word *Abba* is only used in Mark, and then only in the intimacy of Jesus' prayer in Gethsemane. Of course, such a highly charged emotional situation would be precisely the kind of circumstance in which a bilingual person would naturally use such a word as this from his home language, and probably even from his childhood prayers. It is also possible that, at the time of Jesus or later, this word *abba* became almost a technical term. Or it may, because of its use by Jesus in the Garden of Gethsemane, have passed into Christian usage without translation, as did the word *Amen* (cf. Paul's usage in Galatians iv. 6.)

Similarly the words from the Cross would naturally be in the "home language" of Aramaic. Indeed, anyone acquainted with bilingualism would expect no other pattern. But the remainder of the "Aramaic *logia*" supplied by Jeremias fall into a different category. Although it has been argued above that the word *passover* had become a technical term common in Hellenistic Judaism, its use in the Gospels is interesting. It never occurs on Jesus' lips in the Fourth Gospel. In the synoptic Gospels Jesus never uses it outside the circle of the Disciples, again a situation in which the use of Aramaic would be natural.

The words *bar* and *Boanerges* are similarly restricted. An analysis of the word *Gehenna* is also interesting. It occurs only once in Mark, and this in Jesus' reply to John (ix. 43 ff.) In Luke (xii. 5) Jesus again uses *Gehenna* once in warning the Disciples against the leaven of the Pharisees. Matthew, however, uses *Gehenna* six times (v. 22 and 29, x. 28, xviii. 9, xxiii. 15 and xxiii. 33). He uses it twice in the Sermon on the Mount, twice in teaching to the Disciples, and twice in the woes to the Scribes and Pharisees.

Gehenna may have become a technical term even for

Greek-speaking Jews, as also might the word *Mammon*. This latter word occurs four times in the Gospels: Matthew includes it in the Sermon on the Mount, but Luke only uses it in the context of the teaching to the Disciples, where it would be natural for such an Aramaic word to occur. As to the words *raca* and *sata*, the first only occurs once in the New Testament, in Matthew v. 22; the second occurs only twice, once again in Matthew, xiii. 33, and once in Luke, xiii. 21. It is interesting to note that whilst Matthew places *sata* in a parable of the Kingdom of Heaven, Luke places it in a teaching situation in a synagogue. Mark never uses this Aramaic word for *measure* on Jesus' lips, but prefers the Greek word *metron*.

The use of the word/technical term *rabbi* is also interesting and somewhat complex. This word would certainly be a technical term well known to Hellenistic Jews. Only in Matthew is the word used by Jesus, in xxiii. 8, and, as mentioned above, Jesus rejects it. Judas Iscariot uses the word in both Matthew and Luke, and Peter uses it twice in Mark. In John the use of the word *rabbi* is both unusual and consistent. There this title is given to Jesus by the two disciples of John the Baptist (i. 38), by Nathanael (i. 49), by Nicodemus (iii. 2), again by the disciples of John the Baptist (iii. 26) and finally by the crowd which followed Jesus to Capernaum (vi. 25). It seems hardly coincidental that in each case in this Gospel the title is given to Jesus by people who, apparently, are seeking to make Jesus' acquaintance or wish to follow him.

Concerning *Beelzebul*: in both Mark iii. 22 and Luke xi. 15 ff. and in parallels in Matthew, this word/name is in each instance introduced into conversation by someone other than Jesus. After this word has been brought into the conversation by his opponents Jesus uses it in reply in Matthew and Luke. More often, however, Jesus seems to prefer to use the word *Satan*, which quite possibly was a more common usage amongst Hellenistic Jews. In Matthew and

Luke Jesus introduces the word *Satan* before using the word *Beelzebul*, which his opponents have previously introduced. It is possible that for some of his hearers *Beelzebul* would have no meaning, whereas the Graecized *Satan* would be understandable by all. In Matthew x.25, Jesus does introduce the word *Beelzebul*, but this is in the context of the teaching to the Disciples. In the Markan version of this instance, Jesus uses the word *Satan*. All these seem to indicate that although the name *Satan* was a common one amongst the Greek-speaking Jews, its use in the Gospels is sparing indeed. Again, in the Gospel according to S[t] John, this name is never found on Jesus' lips. Apart from the reply to his opponents, the name *Satan* is used in all three synoptic Gospels in the account of the Temptations. Jesus uses it to Peter in Matthew and Mark at Caesarea Philippi, and in Luke at the Last Supper. In Luke also, Jesus uses it in connection with the Seventy, and in the synagogue. In Mark, Jesus uses it in the Parable of the Sower.

Similarly the use of the word *sabbath* is severely limited on the lips of Jesus. John allows Jesus to use it only once, and that in the Temple (vii. 22). In Matthew, Jesus uses the word four times in chapter xii. In verses 5 and 8 he uses it to the Pharisees after they have introduced it, and in verses 11 and 12 he uses it in the synagogue in similar circumstances. In xxiv. 20 Jesus also uses *sabbath* in speaking to the Disciples. In Mark (ii. 24 ff.) it is introduced by the Pharisees, and in Mark iii. 4 Jesus uses it in the synagogue. The pattern is similar in Luke, with the addition of its use in the house of a Pharisee, in chapter xiv. 3 and 5.

To summarize: apart from the name *Cephas*, Jesus is recorded as using only one other Aramaic word in the Gospel according to S[t] John, and that is the word *sabbath*. If the Graecized words of *passover, rabbi, sabbath* and *Satan* are excluded, Mark and Luke record no Aramaic word used by Jesus in the context of the teaching of the people. All other Aramaic words used by Jesus in these two Gospels are used either in personal prayer, in the home situation, in the discipleship groups, or are introduced by Jesus' opponents. This accords exactly with bilingual practice. Even if the four common words which have been Graecized are included, only once, and that in the case of *Satan* in the Parable of the Sower, is an Aramaic word used outside those contexts in which it would be natural for a bilingual speaker to use Aramaic. This consistency indicates how careful is the use of their material by Mark and Luke, and how restricted is the use to which Aramaic was put by Jesus in his teaching ministry. Matthew is not so careful, and although his use of Aramaic words is limited, because his account of much of Jesus' teaching is gathered into large sections such as the Sermon on the Mount he does allow Jesus to use a small number of Aramaic words in the context of his general teaching. An analysis of the use of Aramaic words in the Gospels will be found in Appendix C.

As has been stated before, this thesis does not deny Jesus' use of Aramaic, or even of Hebrew; on the contrary, it recognizes and requires Jesus' use of Aramaic. What it does claim is that the evidence not only suggests, but demands, that Jesus also used the Greek vernacular. He and his followers were bilingual, speaking in family and in fellowship groups in their "home" language, but speaking, and in Jesus' case teaching, in the larger world, in Greek. The Aramaic hypothesis, and it is only that, is revealed as a most unlikely hypothesis. There was no need for Aramaic originals of the Gospels, or for a peculiarly Aramaic phase in the development of the Church's scriptures. The Palestinian-Jewish Christians had no need for such a phase: they could speak and read Greek. But the Hellenistic Jew and the Gentile equally demanded an immediate use of Greek for their understanding of the teachings of Jesus. It is exceedingly unlikely that, even if the Palestinian Jewish Christians would have liked the teachings of Jesus written down in their "home" language, there would have been time or energy to construct such a scripture. The pressures of the Greek-speaking demand would have been too great.

In bilingual situations words move from one language to another in both directions. It is sometimes amusing, when listening to Welsh people speaking Welsh, to hear, in the midst of a flow of Welsh words, such English words as *television*, *ambulance* and *paint*, introduced into the conversation. It is even more amusing, as the present writer has heard, when the speaker endeavours to give an English word a Welsh sound as, for instance, when asking in a shop for "painteo".

Similarly, some Greek words were adopted by the Jews, and made very much a part of their religion and culture. Reference will be made in the next chapter to the Greek word *synagogue*, but that word is not alone in attaining prominence in the Jewish world. *Sanhedrin* is another Greek word adopted by the Jews and given a position of importance in the early years of the Christian era, as is the name *Pentecost*. One of the most interesting of such words is the name "Zealot", a member of which group was, apparently, numbered amongst Jesus' disciples. It is so easy to assume that the nationalistic Zealots were anti-Hellenistic, but this is not so. Their nationalism was directed against the occupying Romans.

The name Zealot comes from the Greek word *zelos*, meaning jealousy, enmity or rebellion. The Zealots were a branch of the Saducean sect, and always supported Herod the Great. When the Romans annexed Judaea, the members of this sect were proud to describe themselves as Herodians. S[t] Luke twice indicates in the Acts of the Apostles that the Disciples were all Galileans. (i. 11 and ii. 7) In view of this it is interesting to observe that the headquarters of the Zealots were in the cities of Galilee; another indication of the penetration of Hellenistic culture and its accompanying bilingualism.

In fact, at the turn of the millennium not all Jews were by any means so "exclusive" as many scholars would suggest. An example of late-first-century-B.C. Jewish catholicity is seen in the fact that Marcus Agrippa was permitted to sacrifice one hundred oxen in the still-unfinished Court of the Gentiles. One of the Temple gates was named after him, and Philo writes about the enthusiasm inspired by his diplomatic action. Philo says, "He was escorted as far as the harbour, not just by a single city, but by the whole country, while branches were strewn in his path." It seems that the populace of Jerusalem had precedents for the enthusiastic behaviour at Jesus' triumphal entry into their city.

CHAPTER V

Jesus and the Synagogue

Writing about the Synagogue and its worship, Rabbi L. Rabinowitz said,

> Before passing to a discussion of the homily, a word must be said about the translation into the vernacular (Aramaic). The interpreter stood at the side of the person reading the Law, and more or less freely, paraphrased the reading, sometimes erring on the side of a too great literalness, sometimes on the side of too great freedom.[75]

The implication of this statement is, of course, that this is how the worship of a synagogue took place in the time of Jesus. Because this statement is made by a Jewish Rabbi who, we at first assume, is an expert on the subject, we take note with almost reverent awe: until, in fact, we realize that this is sheer speculation. It is not until the matter is really investigated that it is learnt how little, in fact, is known about the synagogue, or its worship, in first century Palestine. A quotation from W. O. E. Oesterley is very revealing. He writes:

> It is generally held that the *synagogue, as an institution*, came into being during the Exile. While this was probably the case, it must be recognized that there is no evidence available for the existence of synagogues in Palestine prior to the second century B.C. In the Dispersion the earliest mention of them is in the reign of Ptolemy Euergetes, King of Egypt 247–221 B.C.[76]

Synagogue, to most people, is such a Jewish term that it is rather surprising to recall, as Oesterley says, that

> The word "synagogue" is Greek, meaning assembly (= the Hebrew *Beth ha Keneseth,* "*House of Assembly*"); no Hebrew or Aramaic term for it occurs in the Old or New Testament; the mention in Psalm lxxiv 8 (English version) of "synagogue" or "places of assembly" refers, as the context shows, to assemblies or festivals held in the Temple courts; hence the Septuagint rendering "feasts of the Lord".[77]

Rabinowitz knows of the sparsity of the evidence, of course, for he says, "the first coherent accounts of the synagogue services are to be found in the New Testament (Luke iv and Acts xiii)."

Meyers and Strange, consequent upon their archaeological excavations, support this statement. They write,

> Both Josephus and a contemporary scholar number the synagogues of first-century Jerusalem in the hundreds, but apart from the Theodotus inscription discussed earlier, there is virtually no archeological trace of them. What we have in this instance is a problem of terminology that needs clarification both here and in scholarly literature. Although the Greek term *synagogue* connotes a place of assembly, as does its Semitic equivalent, it sheds no light whatever on the physical nature of what was thought to be such an assembly place. The primary functions of a synagogue were prayer and study, hence the terms *beth tefilah* (house of prayer) or *beth midrash* (house of study). It is highly likely, therefore, that in the period when the Temple still stood, a synagogue could well have been nothing more than a large meeting room in a private house, or part of a larger structure set apart for worship. If this were the case, then the argument for house-churches at Capernaum and elsewhere

becomes all the more compelling.[78]

They continue:

> When the Jewish population of Judaea and Samaria began to establish themselves in Galilee after the Roman wars, one of the first problems was the issue of how and where to pray. On the basis of archeological evidence from more than one hundred ancient Palestinian synagogues, however, it is difficult to date the earliest evidences of synagogues before the mid-third century C.E. [that is, in Meyers-and-Strange terminology, the "Christian era".] The import of this data is quite clear, namely, it took a century or more for these newly established communities to accumulate sufficient means to build public places of worship in which they invested not only considerable funds but even more their hopes and wishes for a better future in the richly variegated architectural monuments of the talmudic period.[79]

This statement of Meyers and Strange confirms how little is known of the life and worship of the synagogue during the life-time of Jesus, and indicates how speculative is the Rabinowitz statement, and his subsequent description of synagogue worship. It must be recalled that by the time any firm evidence of synagogue worship and architecture is available, the split between the Jews and the Christians had long been irrevocable.

The life of the Jews of Galilee in the post-Roman-wars era must have been very different in many respects from that of their ancestors in the opening decades of the first century, and it must be extremely hazardous to assume that conditions at the end of the second century and in the third century A.D., as far as the synagogue was concerned, were similar to those in the lifetime of Jesus of Nazareth. The only evidence that Rabinowitz can supply for his conjecture about the translation of Hebrew into Aramaic in the synagogue of first-century Galilee is from the Mishnah. He says, "In Mishnaic times the rule was laid down that every verse was translated singly and separately by the Meturgeman (Translator), in the case of the prophets every three verses."[80]

Rabinowitz gives no Mishnaic reference for his claim, but it is found in Megillah iv. 4, which says, "He that reads in the Law may not read less than three verses; he may not read to the interpreter ["from the Hebrew into the Aramaic speech of the unlearned," according to a footnote] more than one verse, or, in (a reading from) the Prophets, three verses." This statement, however, should be read in conjunction with other statements in the same Megillah section of the Mishnah. As has already been quoted above, Rabban Simeon b. Gamaliel said that the Books (the Scriptures) had only been permitted to be written in Greek as well as Hebrew (Megillah i. 8) and in Megillah ii. 1 it says, "But it [the Scripture] may be read in a foreign tongue to them that speak a foreign tongue." In all this discussion, however, it must be constantly borne in mind that the Mishnah is of the late second century A.D.

The fact of the matter is that no one knows what, for instance, the synagogue at Nazareth was really like, nor what pattern of worship took place there, apart from the very sparse account given in St Luke iv. 16–28. The synagogue itself could have been no more than a room in a house set aside for regular meetings. All that can be said about the form of worship on the occasion described in St Luke is that it included a reading from the book of the Prophet Isaiah, which was followed by a homily. What if this synagogue was, as Meyers and Strange suggest that some were, a *beth midrash*—a house of study? We must not assume that synagogues were the same while the Temple was the centre of Jewish worship as they were after the destruction of the Temple. Furthermore, we must also recall that Jewish (and Islamic) spirituality is of a very different nature from that of Christian spirituality. It is not known if corporate prayer was a part of synagogue life while the Temple was a place of prayer; we have simply assumed that it was. It is interesting to note that there is no reference to prayer at all in respect of the synagogue in Mark, Luke, John or the Acts of the Apostles. The only reference to prayer in the synagogue in the Gospels and in Acts is in Matthew vi. 5. Even here the reference seems to be to individual and ostentatious prayer rather than to prayer in the context of corporate worship, for the text says, "And when you pray, you must not be like the hypocrites: for they love to stand and pray in the synagogues and at street corners, that they may be seen of men."

Indeed, all the references to the synagogues of the synoptic Gospels and the Acts of the Apostles (the references in the Gospel according to S[t] John are few; nevertheless they are consistent with the synoptics) suggest the *beth midrash* (house of study) rather than the *beth tefilah* (house of prayer). Jesus' activity there, and later, Paul's, is exclusively reading the Scriptures, preaching, teaching and healing—the last causing considerable antipathy. Another aspect of the synagogue which comes through from the New Testament accounts is their function as a court which could punish and ostracize. In all the references to Jesus' preaching and teaching in the synagogues in the Gospels, no mention is ever made of his use of an interpreter, or of interpreting the reading himself, in the sense of translating from one language to another.

If the common ignorance of Hebrew was as great as New Testament scholars insist, and if there were as many synagogues (no doubt some very small in the country villages—in fact the Mishnah speaks of synagogues with less than ten men) as both the Gospels and Josephus suggest (hundreds in Jerusalem alone) the implication must be that the job of translator must have been the most popular one in Palestinian Judaism at that time. It also must be asked why, if it was possible to train so many translators (and the ability to translate by ear must imply a greater expertise in a language than simply reading that language) the Hebrew language had fallen into such desuetude amongst ordinary people. If there were so many teachers of Hebrew about, to train all these translators, why did they not hold classes to teach Hebrew to the ordinary people? Furthermore, why bother to train countless men in understanding and translating Hebrew when a perfectly good Greek translation of the Scriptures was available to them which, for the vast majority, would need no translation? Once again, the inconsistencies (one is almost tempted to say, the imbecilities) of the Aramaic hypothesis become apparent.

Contemporary students are apt not to realize the venerability of the Septuagint in the time of Jesus' ministry. Because the study of the Old Testament history involves the consideration of so vast a period, beginning with echoes of the Hammurabic Code (c. 2000 B.C.) through the Hyksos period (c. 1750 B.C.), through the time of the Exodus, the Judges, the establishment of the Kingdom, the destruction of the Northern kingdom, the Exile and the subsequent Return, we are apt to think that, for the Jew of Jesus' day, the production of the Septuagint was a relatively recent event. *Relatively* recent is right. Nevertheless, the Septuagint was very venerable. It needs to be remembered that the time span between the production of the Septuagint and the ministry of Jesus was over three hundred years. That is a period half as long again as the United States of America has been an independent nation. It is almost as long a period as that which separates the present-day Church of England from the publication of the 1662 Book of Common Prayer. For some one like Peter or Andrew the Septuagint would probably have first appeared in the days of their great, great, great, great, great, great, great grandfathers. That is venerability, and in a society and culture which so venerated venerability, the Septuagint would have achieved a very significant status by the time of the ministry of Jesus.

With the widespread use of Greek in Galilee, with the venerability of the Septuagint, and with the problems with the translator situation which Rabinowitz' hypothesis would present, it is highly probable that the version of the Scriptures read in the synagogue in Nazareth, and especially in Capernaum, would be the Septuagint. Eusebius believed that it was the version used by the Disciples of Jesus, if not by Jesus himself.[81]

For over two centuries certain scholars have endeavoured to persuade the mass of their New Testament colleagues to look at the evidence; but scholarly prejudice is as difficult to overcome as any other kind of prejudice. In 1767 Diodati published *De Christo Graece Loquenti* in Naples, and this was reprinted by Dobbin of London nearly a century and a half ago, in 1843. In 1850 E. W. Grinfield published *An Apology for the Septuagint* in London. He was convinced that Jesus grew up, both at home and in the local synagogue, nurtured on the Septuagint. Although some of his reasons for this conviction would now only be acceptable to those who hold a fundamentalist-literalist position about the Bible, much of the evidence he supplies is accurate and weighty. He argues that when Jesus went into the synagogue at Nazareth he would have used the Septuagint, because the passage in Luke iv. 18 and 19 is almost *verbatim* from the Septuagint. He says that if Jesus had read from the Hebrew, not a single individual would have understood him, and it could not "have been fulfilled in their ears". Perhaps more importantly, Grinfield says:

> Out of the thirty-seven quotations made by Jesus himself from the Old Testament, thirty-three agree almost verbatim with the LXX, two agree with the Hebrew and differ from the LXX, one differs from both, and one partially agrees with both. Only six agree exactly

with the Hebrew. From this enumeration, it is plain, that our Lord constantly used and quoted the version.[82]

Of course, the overwhelming use of the Septuagint in the synoptic Gospels cannot provide completely conclusive evidence that Jesus spoke Greek, although it gives such an hypothesis strong support. What is more, the question must be asked: Why, if there were original Aramaic documents upon which the Gospels are based, did the Evangelists choose to quote from the Septuagint version? Another consequent question is: Were these Septuagint quotations in the hypothetical original Aramaic documents? If they were, then presumably they were in Greek, and this would make the Aramaic documents themselves an exercise in bilingualism. If these documents were themselves bilingual, what was the point of producing a bilingual document if the readers already understood Greek? These questions demand answers, for it must be appreciated that if these hypothetical original documents were not bilingual, then the situation becomes exceedingly complex. Either, in the hypothetical documents, the quotations from the Old Testament were in Hebrew, which the Evangelists, for some inexplicable reason of their own, extracted, substituting for them the Septuagint quotations, or else, in these same hypothetical original documents, the original quotations were Jesus' own Aramaic translations of the Hebrew text, with which the Evangelists dispensed, in order to replace them with the Septuagint text. When the care (illustrated above) with which Mark and Luke appear to record the few Aramaic sayings of Jesus is appreciated, it seems highly unlikely that these same Evangelists would jettison Jesus' Aramaic translations in favour of the Septuagint version of the Scriptures. Once more it becomes apparent how devious the explanations have to be for the Aramaic hypothesis to retain any credibility whatsoever.

The Acts of the Apostles supports the thesis that it was

the Septuagint version which was widely used in Palestine in the first century A.D. In the incident concerning the Ethiopian eunuch it can hardly be suggested that this man in viii. 32 was reading anything other than the Septuagint. To argue otherwise would again involve the construction of yet another unlikely hypothesis, that he had chosen to learn Hebrew first. But our evidence above has shown that bilingualism was very widespread in Jerusalem, and he would know that he would have no difficulty in communicating there in Greek. It is also interesting to note that the word *Ethiopian* is used in the Septuagint for descendants of Cush.

It would be interesting to ask what was the version that was read in the synagogue in Damascus. It can only have been the Septuagint, and this would indicate the probability of the Greek Gospel long before, as Manson suggested, one was required in Antioch. It would also seem that although Paul could speak Hebrew, he naturally used the Septuagint. His whole argument in Acts xiii depends upon quotations from the Septuagint. Even more significant is the fact that though James, at the Council of Jerusalem, as recorded in Acts xv, uses the most Semitic form of Peter's name, he quotes the Scripture from the Septuagint. Indeed, his argument depends upon variants peculiar to the Septuagint. Again, unless Luke was involved in convoluted substitutions, James, the most Judaistic of the leaders of the early Church, was not averse to using the Septuagint, rather than the Hebrew text. What is even more important is that this implied that James was bilingual: and if James was, why was not Jesus?

There is other evidence also not only of Paul's preference for the Septuagint, but of his reliance upon it. In his Epistle to the Galatians (and even the most radical New Testament critic would hardly deny Pauline authorship here) he quotes Genesis xii. 3 (Galatians iii. 8) from the Septuagint version. In Galatians iii. 19 Paul refers to the tradition that angels were present at the giving of the Law. This tradition is not in the original Hebrew, but is preserved in the Septuagint. (Cf. Acts vii. 38 and 53, Hebrews ii. 2, Book of Jubilees i, and Josephus, Antiquities xv. 3⁸³.) All this evidence shows how widespread and influential the Septuagint version had become by the first century A.D.

Grinfield also makes some other noteworthy points. Arguing that Jesus would have been instructed by his parents from the Septuagint, he claims that the Magnificat, the Benedictus and the Annunciation to Mary, are all recorded in Septuagintal language. He also claims that when Jesus put the Scribes and Pharisees to silence by the argument from Psalm cx. 1 (Mark xii. 36 and parallels), he adopted the Septuagint so literally that what is said could hardly apply to the Hebrew text at all. From this he infers that those who "sat on Moses' seat" did not object to the quotation being taken from the Greek version.

Grinfield gives an interesting extract from an article which appeared in *The Quarterly Journal of Prophecy* for October, 1848. It is entitled "Quotations by our Lord from the Old Testament". It is reproduced below. Apart from a few minor points, it is compatible with the comments in standard contemporary commentaries.

QUOTATIONS BY OUR LORD FROM THE OLD TESTAMENT

Matthew

iv. 4; Luke iv. 4 ... ... agrees verbatim with the Septuagint
iv. 6 (by Satan) ... ... taken from the Septuagint
iv. 7 ... ... verbatim with the Septuagint
iv. 10 ... ... taken from the Septuagint
ix. 13,* xii. 7 ... ... verbatim from the Septuagint
xi. 10; Mark i. 2; Luke vii. 27 ... differs from both Hebrew and the Septuagint
xiii. 14, 15; Mark iv. 12;
      Luke viii. 10 ... taken from the Septuagint
xv. 8, 9 ... ... differs from the Hebrew, agrees with the Septuagint
xix. 5 ... ... taken from the Septuagint
xix. 18, 19 ... ... verbatim with the Septuagint
xxi. 13; Mark xi. 17;
    Luke xix. 46 ... ... agrees with both Hebrew and Septuagint. Bloomfield on Mark; Govett on Isaiah lvi. Not mentioned by Horne
xix. 19, xxii. 39 ... ... verbatim with the Septuagint
xxi. 16 ... ... verbatim with the Septuagint
xxii. 42; Mark xii. 10;
      Luke xx. 37 ... verbatim with the Septuagint
xxii. 37; Mark xii. 30; Luke x. 27 ... agrees with the Septuagint in sense not in words; nearly agrees with the Hebrew
xxii. 44; Mark xii. 36
      Luke xx. 42 ... ... verbatim with the Septuagint
xxvi. 31 ... ... verbatim with the Septuagint
xxvii. 46 (in Hebrew) ... ... differs from Septuagint; agrees with the Hebrew

Luke

iv. 18, 19; xxii. 37 ... ... agrees in sense, not words, with the Septuagint. Exact with the Hebrew

---

* But Moses Stuart says this is a direct translation from the Hebrew.

CHAPTER VI

The Use of Greek in the Post-Resurrection Period

The Acts of the Apostles uses the Greek word *synagogue* more than any other book in the New Testament. *Synagogue* occurs nineteen times in Acts compared with fifteen in the Gospel according to S[t] Luke. Together, Luke/Acts uses this word more often than all the other New Testament books put together. (Matthew nine times, Mark eight, John two and Revelation two.) In addition to this Greek word which has penetrated so deeply into Judaism, Acts demonstrates that two other Greek words became of fundamental importance to the Jewish faith and race. Acts introduces the name Pentecost (used otherwise in the New Testament only in 1 Corinthians xvi. 8) and uses the word *Sanhedrin* more frequently than any other New Testament book. (Matthew three times, Mark three, Luke and John one each.) Foakes Jackson and Lake, in their five-volume commentary on Acts,[84] say that the word *Sanhedrin* was taken up by the Jews into rabbinic language, and that the Council was henceforth known as the Sanhedrin. Here again is a profound illustration of how deeply the Greek language had penetrated into first-century Judaism.

It has been pointed out above (pp. 69 ff.) that there are Greek names amongst those of the Twelve. One of the disciples who is said to have accompanied Jesus on the walk to

Emmaus also had a Graecized name. In Acts iv. 6, one of the two important men associated with the high priests Annas and Caiaphas has a Greek name, to wit, Alexander. As has been mentioned above, all of the Seven (Acts vi. 5) have Greek names. In Acts ix. 33 Peter heals a man with the thoroughly Greek name, Aeneas. In xii. 13 the servant girl in the house of Mary of Jerusalem has the Greek name Rhoda. According to Josephus, the father of the high priest Ananias (Acts xxiii. 2) was the son of a man with the Greek name Nebadaeus.

There is a great deal of evidence concerning Greek-speaking Jews of the post-resurrection era. John Mark, the son of Mary of Jerusalem, in whose house the early Church met, had a Latin name, and could almost certainly speak Greek. It is indisputable that Paul and Barnabas could speak Greek. C. E. B. Cranfield's hint[85] that Peter spoke only Aramaic until old age, is quite untenable. That an intelligent Galilean Jew, born and brought up in a bilingual area, brother of a man with a Greek name, engaged in commerce (presumably he had to sell his fish as well as catch them), in a predominantly Gentile part of Galilee; a leader in the post-resurrection Church which quickly had a preponderance of Greek-speaking Jews as its members; who initiated the Gentile mission, conversing with, converting and ordering to be baptized, a Gentile, Greek-speaking Roman centurion of the Italian band (Acts x. 1 ff.); who spent some time in Greek-speaking Antioch, eating with Gentiles (Galatians ii. 11) and, apparently, spending some years in cosmopolitan Rome, with Greek-speaking Mark as his companion, would spend his life locked in Aramaic isolation, is so banal a theory that it would never have been considered if it were not for the incredible but quite unfounded strength of the Aramaic hypothesis.

Furthermore, unless most of the Twelve were bilingual, the tradition which says that certain of the first Disciples journeyed to different parts of the world, preaching the

Gospel, must be dismissed as pure fiction. If they were not already bilingual they would have to have learnt Greek. If they were bilingual, they would have had no problem in communicating the Gospel in vast areas of the then known world.

There is still more evidence for the bilingualism of the early followers of Jesus in the Acts of the Apostles. Unless the Pentecostal tongues of Acts ii was not an example of glossolalia, but was a miraculous and simultaneous translation of Peter's words into different languages, many of the people present would not have understood Peter's sermon which followed the outpouring of the Holy Spirit, if it had been spoken in Aramaic, for, indisputably, many were Greek-speaking Jews. Furthermore, there is no indication either that Peter's sermon was of a glossolalian character or in Aramaic. On the contrary, it was a reasonable, rational statement, intended to reach, interest, inform and convert as many as possible. If Peter had been speaking Aramaic most of his audience would have been baffled.

Acts vi indicates how early Greek-speaking Jews became part of the Church. This must have involved inter-communication between the two groups, and hence a considerable degree of bilingualism. As mentioned above, Stephen's speech, with its numerous quotations from the Septuagint, must strongly dispose us towards the belief that he was most likely a Hellenistic Jew who, again most probably, would not speak Aramaic anyway. It is at the death of Stephen that Saul/Paul first comes on to the New Testament scene. Could it be that Paul was a member of that synagogue where Stephen first came into conflict with his fellow Jews? In Acts vi. 9 that synagogue is said to contain those of Cilicia, and Paul was a native of Cilicia. (Acts xxi. 39, xxii 3; and Galatians i. 21)

Similarly, Stephen's colleague amongst the Seven, Philip, must have been Greek-speaking, for he would have needed that language to expound the Gospel to the Ethiopian eunuch. (Acts viii. 28 ff.) As has been stated above, because the name Philip is a Greek name there is a predisposition to consider the Philip who was one of the Seven as a Jew of the Dispersion. This, of course, may not be so, for Philip the Apostle was Galilean, and, similarly, the other Philip might have been a Palestinian. Whether he was a Palestine Jew or a Jew of the Dispersion, Philip of the Seven seems to have had no inhibitions about preaching the Gospel in places other than Jerusalem. In fact, he seems to have had a strong inclination towards the Hellenistic centres in Palestine. He preached in the old Samaria, which was in Philip's time the magnificent Greek Sebaste. Similarly, he preached in Azotus, the old Philistine city of Ashdod; in the cities of the coastland which contained large Gentile, Greek-speaking populations; and he finally settled in Caesarea, the Roman capital of the province of Judaea. Here Paul, and presumably Luke also, stayed with Philip, where he lived with his four daughters who, it seems, were both virgins and prophets. (Acts xxi. 8) (This is one of the "we" passages, so it may be assumed that Luke was at this point accompanying Paul.)

Peter seems to a degree to have followed in Philip's footsteps, for Acts ix. 31 and 32 suggests that he travelled through Judaea, Galilee and Samaria. He eventually reached Lydda, and it is possible that Philip also had some contact with this particular Church. Here, of course, Peter healed the sick man Aeneas. It is this particular journey which leads Peter to one of the most significant events both of his life and of that of the early Church, his contact with the Greek-speaking Gentile centurion, Cornelius.

It is interesting to note that this centurion bears the name of a great Roman house. It was not, however, only Peter who came and had conversation with the household of Cornelius. He was accompanied by others from Joppa, who also must have been Greek-speaking, for they shared Peter's astonishment when the Holy Spirit fell on the Gentiles. It is true that the companions of Peter heard the Gentiles "speaking with tongues", but also they heard them "extolling God", which presumably they would not have recognized if they did not understand the language in which the Gentiles were speaking. Furthermore, when Peter reported back to the Circumcision party, he explained how the six brethren went with him and heard about the angel's message to Cornelius. (Acts xi. 12, 13) Again, it is difficult to understand how this information could have been shared if they had not the bond of a common language.

This same chapter of Acts goes on to say how "those who were scattered because of the persecution that arose over Stephen travelled as far as Phoenicia, Cyprus and Antioch." Some of these, apparently, were men who were Jews of the Dispersion, for "some of them [were] men of Cyprus and Cyrene, who on coming to Antioch spoke to the Gentiles." It may be that those who spoke "the Word to none except Jews" were Palestinian Jews. Whether they were or not, all, apparently, could speak Greek.

A prophet from Jerusalem, a travelling teacher, must also have been able to speak Greek, or would have had to bring his interpreter with him. Agabus, with other prophets from Jerusalem, foretold the coming of a famine. This prophecy took place in Antioch, and must have been spoken in Greek. It seems likely that Agabus' companions spoke Greek; for there would have been little point in sending them down from Jerusalem if they did not. (Acts xi. 27ff.) Furthermore, Acts xv. 1 indicates that other Palestinian Christian Jews travelled to Antioch in an attempt to controvert the teaching of Paul and Barnabas, demanding that the Gentile Christians be circumcized. Once again, these Jewish Christians, who were very committed to certain aspects of Judaism, must have been Greek-speaking, for there would have been little point in going down to try to win Gentiles to their point of view if they could not communicate with them.

Again, after the subsequent Council of Jerusalem, when

the Apostles and the Elders wanted to send a message back to Antioch with Paul and Barnabas, they chose two "leading men of the brethren". One of these was Judas, called Barsabbas, and the other was Silas. The first had a thoroughly Hebraist name, and he may have been the brother of Joseph Barsabbas. The second had a Latin name, Silas, and most likely was a Roman citizen; see Acts xvi. 37. This also indicates the close relationship between some Jewish Christians of Palestine, and those of the Dispersion. Judas must have been Greek-speaking, whilst Silas had become a leading figure amongst the brethren. Both of them spent some time in Antioch "exhorting the brethren with many words" which Judas would have found difficulty in doing if he did not speak Greek.

In the later chapters of the Acts of the Apostles there is considerable evidence that the Jewish leaders in Jerusalem were bilingual. It is difficult to see how they would have understood the tribune, Claudias Lysias, in the controversy over Paul (Acts xxi. 32 and 33) or he them, if they were not. It is evident from Lysias' astonishment at Paul's ability to speak Greek (Acts xxi. 37) that he, Lysias, did not speak Aramaic. Similarly, Ananias the High Priest and his companions (Acts xxiv. 1 ff.) would hardly have journeyed to appear before Felix if they were unable to speak to the governor in Greek. Although Felix had a Jewish wife, there is no reason to suppose that being married to Drusilla (the daughter of Herod Agrippa I, the ruler who had killed James the Apostle) would have prompted him to learn Aramaic. He had after all been married twice before. It could be argued that the Jews took Tertullus with them as a spokesman because they were not very adept in the Greek tongue. Tertullus was most probably, however, the professional lawyer and, in any case, the Jews would not have been able to brief him if they were not bilingual.

The evidence, therefore, that Jerusalem at the time of

Jesus, and in the years of the early Church, was a thoroughly cosmopolitan city, seems overwhelming. In such a city most people would use Greek as the general means of communication. From the evidence set out above, it is apparent that the early Church most probably used Greek as their main medium of communication right from the beginning; and if they did there is little reason to suppose that they bothered to produce written Aramaic accounts of the life and teaching of Jesus, when so many members of the infant Church were perfectly able to speak and understand Greek.

On the contrary, what evidence there is seems to suggest that Aramaic was comparatively little written in first-century Palestine. Archaeological evidence points to a paucity of written Aramaic of the first century A.D. It is perhaps significant that Josephus apparently abandoned his original intention to publish his work in Aramaic, and wrote in Greek instead. All the first-century Christian documents known to have existed were written in Greek. Origen (185–254 A.D.) mentions the discovery of Greek and Hebrew manuscripts found stored in jars in Jericho, and it is possible that he used material from these manuscripts for his production of the Hexapla.

It is interesting to note that written Aramaic seems to have experienced something of a revival from the second century onwards. As mentioned above (p. 20), Jeremias has to use the Palestinian Talmud and Midrashim of the fourth century A.D. as his evidence for the Aramaic hypothesis. The earliest Jewish Targums were most probably written in the second century, and the Syrian (Peshitta) version probably appeared at the end of the second century (see page 37 above). A. R. Burn, writing in *The Pelican History of Greece*, says, "In the Roman east, Greek remained the language of civilization; native languages such as 'the speech of Lycaonia', Galatian, Aramaic, were spoken, but comparatively little written."[86] Burn also goes on to point out that the

Greek Church was slow to translate the New Testament into Aramaic, and that the first versions in Syriac (eastern Aramaic) were made east of the Euphrates, outside the Empire. These could not have been made before the second century.

Burn makes another interesting comment which contradicts the picture of Jewish intellectual separation from Hellenism so beloved by many New Testament scholars. He writes,

> Seleucid Antioch had its royal library, and as late as the last century B.C. there arose a school of Syro-Greek poets, who wrote their short elegiac love-poems, occasional poems and epitaphs with a voluptuous sweetness reminiscent of the Song of Songs. ...Meleagros of Gadara, in the Decapolis, the ten towns east of Jordan (Greek towns—hence the Gadarene swine, an abomination to the Jews), the best of these poets also collected the first nucleus of our Greek Anthology of such "epigrams". He called it his *Garland* and, in an introductory poem, compared the work of each author to a different flower with the famous phrase "of Sappho few, but roses".[87]

Similarly, the statement by Charles F. Pfeifer would discomfit the same New Testament scholars when he writes, of the Dead Sea Scrolls,

> The Essenes believed in immortality; they rejected the doctrine of bodily resurrection. The question of outside influences on Essenism is an interesting one, but we may note here that this denial of resurrection is probably to be related to the Greek philosophical concept of the evil of matter.[88]

To return to the hypothesis that little Aramaic was written during the first century A.D., but that there was a revival of this activity from the second century onwards: it is significant to note that the writing down of the Torah and

Oral Law did not take place until after the destruction of the Temple; indeed, the whole purpose of the Mishnah, which appeared in the second half of the second century, was to write down the Torah and Oral Law in Hebrew.

Important support for this hypothesis concerning written Aramaic comes from the Samaritan literature. John Macdonald suggests in his *Theology of the Samaritans* that the *Targum*, the first Aramaic version of the Samaritan Pentateuch, was written in the late third or early fourth century A.D. Macdonald believes that the translation was made by Markah, and goes on to speak about this writer's other major work, *Memar*. This work, says Macdonald, is

> by far the most important Samaritan document after the Pentateuch. It is written in the same Aramaic dialect as the literal *Targum*... it can be dated to the late third century or early fourth centuries A.D. ... *Memar* contains many concepts current only in that time; it shows the first clear traces of the influence of the New Testament. It uses a number of Greek words, but no Latin words, a fact that shows it to have been written at a time long enough after the end of the Hellenistic influence in Palestine for Greek to have fallen out of use as the *lingua franca* of the Near East. Almost all the Greek words used by Markah ceased to be used in literature after his time.[89]

Some other comments by Macdonald are interesting about the opinions of certain New Testament scholars to whom reference has been made immediately above. He writes:

> It seems certain that the Samaritans were considerably influenced by the Greek philosophies that became current in Palestine and Syria at this time. ... The chief mark of Greek philosophy left on the Samaritan mind was in the field of the humanities; we may observe ideas

with Greek affinities on the subject of man, his constitution, purpose, relation to God, and so on. (Markah, in the third or fourth century A.D. seems to reflect the Greek philosophical outlook more than any other writer, and indeed in his great *Memar* [Teaching] he uses several Greek words, where Aramaic words would have served just as well.)[90]

The probability that little Aramaic was written during, at least, the greater part of the first century A.D. seems high. Of course, in respect of this as in so much of our study, empirical testing is impossible. In this, as in the more fundamental question of whether Jesus was monoglotic and restricted to the use of Aramaic, or whether he was bilingual or trilingual, the only satisfactory methodology is to examine all the available historical evidence, carefully, impartially, and comprehensively, and endeavour to reach a balanced conclusion. The fact that the vast majority of New Testament scholars have adhered to the Aramaic hypothesis must not be allowed to stand in the face of historical evidence. If there is a failure to examine the evidence, by the majority, the majority verdict does not guarantee the truth.

To sum up: the two parts of the Aramaic hypothesis are, first, that Jesus spoke only Aramaic, and secondly, that the Greek of the four Gospels seems to suggest an Aramaic background. The first part of this hypothesis is based on the belief that Aramaic was universally spoken in Palestine and, especially in Galilee, was the only language spoken. Now even if this could be demonstrated convincingly, it must be realized that another hypothesis is still required to argue that Jesus was similarly limited. But the evidence cited above shows the overwhelming probability that Greek was a language with a much wider distribution in Palestine than Aramaic. Furthermore, the evidence of the New Testament itself suggests that Jesus spoke Greek. In consequence, this first part of the Aramaic hypothesis just cannot stand.

The evidence for the belief that the Greek of the New Testament has an Aramaic background has been much more thoroughly investigated by New Testament scholars than has the historical background of Aramaic and Greek in the first century A.D. Even if there is an Aramaic background, however, and the present writer is quite ready to accept this possibility, this does not necessarily imply that the people who provided that Aramaic background were restricted to Aramaic, nor does it demand that this Aramaic background necessarily resulted in the production of Aramaic documents. Indeed, the Aramaic background is itself a pointer towards bilingualism and, as has been demonstrated above, the linguistic background to the Gospels by no means rules out bilingualism.

New Testament scholarship, in recent years, has increasingly relied upon hypothesis and circumstantial evidence. It is time to appreciate more fully the limitations of these two elements in research and study. The experience of contemporary criminal court proceedings must reveal the limitations and even the dangers of a too heavy reliance upon circumstantial evidence, especially when it contradicts the evidence of those who give every indication of being reliable witnesses. Of course, every witness can be mistaken; but circumstantial evidence can be both mistaken and unreliable, simply because it can never be known if there is, or was, other evidence which is unavailable for investigation. New Testament scholars have been all too ready to "read between the lines". This may occasionally be useful, but not if this "reading between the lines" contradicts the evidence obtainable from primary witnesses. The basic argument of this work is that the supporters of the Aramaic hypothesis have far too frequently ignored the primary witnesses—a procedure which must invalidate New Testament enquiry.

CHAPTER VII

Conclusion

In conclusion, it may be appropriate to endeavour briefly to assess the significance of the judgement that the Aramaic hypothesis is fatally flawed. This study indicates positively that if Jesus and his followers were bilingual (and all the evidence points to this conclusion), the Evangelists, especially Mark and Luke, took great pains to relate the words Jesus spoke to the context in which they were spoken. On the basis of the structure which Jeremias provides, it is evident that the Evangelists were aware that in some situations (home, discipleship groups, synagogue) Jesus spoke in Aramaic, whilst, in the world at large, he spoke in Greek. A number of important conclusions may be drawn from this.

First, if much of Jesus' teaching to the general public was in Greek, given the faithfulness with which the Evangelists record the context, there is no reason to doubt that much of the teaching of Jesus which we have in the present Greek text is given in the words which Jesus himself used. Secondly, this conclusion should give us confidence in the belief that the carefulness of the Evangelists' work extends to the teaching which Jesus gave in Aramaic. In other words, we can confidently expect that the Greek text is a careful translation of Jesus' Aramaic words. Thirdly, this confidence in the integrity of the Evangelists is reinforced by their rare, but careful, use of actual Aramaic words, and the context in which they are placed. The action of Jesus in speaking to Jairus's daughter in her home language is

CONCLUSION

entirely consistent with the man who declared, "Let the children come to me, do not hinder them; for to such belongs the kingdom of God." (Mark x.14) In this comparatively small way, Jesus' compassion for weaker members of society is clearly indicated. Similarly, the Aramaic words from the Cross give a clear indication of how careful the Evangelists were in reporting what they saw and heard.

In fact, the rejection of the Aramaic hypothesis can open our eyes to the faithfulness of the Gospels, which has been so obscured by much contemporary New Testament scholarship. The acceptance of the belief, indicated by so many aspects of the Gospels, that Jesus could speak their native language, both to those who spoke Aramaic and to those who spoke Greek, makes us take more seriously the real context in which the Gospels were written, and not the theoretical circumstances so beloved of academic theologians.

In the opening pages of this book a quotation was made from J. A. T. Robinson which emphatically but uncritically declared that Jesus taught only in Aramaic. It seems that not long before his death Dr Robinson was revising his opinion. In his book *The Priority of John*, which was edited and published after his death, Robinson says,

> Nicodemus, with his Graecized name, is represented as engaging in a dialogue with Jesus that turns on the double meaning of *anothen* (John iii. 3ff.) which only works in Greek. This cannot of course be used to demonstrate that Jesus actually conversed with him in Greek (though that is entirely possible) but it may well indicate the milieu of the Johannine mission.[91]

In a footnote on the same page he concludes, surprisingly, that:

> Certainly the Roman trial, and many conversations of

Jesus with Pilate, would have been conducted in Greek; and there is no hint in any of the Gospels of an interpreter being necessary.

This, of course, is precisely what is claimed above (p. 53), and is very different from what Robinson said in his book *Can we Trust the New Testament?* If Jesus could speak Greek in Jerusalem, Robinson should have asked himself why Jesus could not also teach in Greek to a people who understood this language.

Robinson was always highly susceptible to ideas from other writers, ideas which he did not always fully understand or digest. His controversial book *Honest to God* was an outstanding example of this trait. In his latter years he was obviously much impressed by the book *John who Saw*, written by a layman, A. H. N. Green-Armytage. It may be that it was the influence of this book which helped Robinson move towards the greater realism revealed in his comments quoted above. Robinson quotes with approval the following passage:

> There is a world—I do not say a world in which all scholars live but one at any rate into which all of them sometimes stray, and which some of them seem permanently to inhabit—which is not the world in which I live. In my world, if *The Times* and *The Telegraph* both tell one story in somewhat different terms, nobody concludes that one of them must have copied the other, nor that the variations in the story have some esoteric significance. But in that world of which I am speaking this would be taken for granted. There, no story is ever derived from facts but always from somebody else's version of the same story.[92]

Green-Armytage refers to only one small element in the vast esoteric fantasia of the scholarly world. Though somewhat inspired by Green-Armytage's words, Robinson cannot

Conclusion

escape from that world, as *The Priority of John* so clearly shows. This posthumously published book is surfeited with the great mass of esoteric theories which abound in the scholarly New Testament world. The purpose of this exercise of examining the Aramaic hypothesis is precisely to challenge that world which Green-Armytage criticizes. It is a world which other ordinary people rarely, if ever, enter, and which exists only within the confines of Academia.

APPENDIX A

The Greek of the New Testament

Some interesting points, relevant to the arguments of this book, are made by N. Turner in an article entitled "The Language of the New Testament".[93]

He begins by stating that anyone whose knowledge of Greek came from the study of Classical authors would not understand the Greek of the New Testament. He traces the descent of New Testament Greek from the old Attic dialect of Athens, but points to the influence of Egypt, for, he claims, the Ptolemaic Empire, with its capital at Alexandria, was the chief centre of the Hellenistic language in the last three centuries B.C.

Turner goes on to state that the language of the New Testament was, in many respects, that of the literary and unliterary *koine* but, he says, "in addition to this the N.T. writers had imported into it the style and (as almost everyone recognises now) the religious context of the Greek Bible." Indeed, he goes on to argue that the Greek of the New Testament is the Greek of the Greek Old Testament which, in turn, is impregnated by Semitic idioms and thought-forms. Consequently, it could be argued that the Aramaic "colouring" of the Greek of the Gospel according to S[t] Mark goes much further back than the language of the author of that Gospel.

Turner then refers to the argument of Professor H. S. Gehman and says,

> Dr Gehman argues persuasively...that in bilingual areas the masses do not keep both languages separate, and there would be a transitional period when Greek-

speaking Jews spoke Greek with "a pronounced Semitic cast". He regards this as temporary...but I would think that many of Jesus' disciples including Paul, were in this bilingual category, that they spoke as well as wrote in this Jewish Greek. It is noteworthy that a well-known specialist in the Greek Old Testament, the Cambridge scholar Dr Peter Katz, has come to a similar conclusion.

Of course, even here there is a considerable element of conjecture, but amongst other positive evidence Katz points to the use of the optative mood. Whilst in other kinds of Greek the optative mood is subject to gradual decay, the opposite is the case in both the Septuagint and the New Testament. Indeed, the frequency of the use in the Septuagint and the New Testament is remarkably similar. Turner says that the optative mood is "well-suited for the lips of pious folk", and he gives as examples Luke i. 38, Romans xv. 5, Romans xv. 13, 1 Thessalonians iii 11 ff., and Hebrews xiii. 20 ff.

APPENDIX B

Analogies and Experiments in Bilingualism

In the international edition of the magazine *The Economist* dated 18–24 August 1984, a book review provided another interesting analogy to the bilingual situation in Palestine in the centuries before and after the birth of Our Lord. The review was of *The New Testament in Scots*, by W. R. Lorimer (Edinburgh, 1984) and the reviewer wrote,

> English, or a variant of it, has been the dominant language in Scotland for about two hundred years, in writing, if not in speech. The loss of political power to London was one of the reasons [this supports the arguments on pp. 34 ff. above] but the death blow to the development of prose in Scotland was the adoption of the Authorized Version of the Bible in English. Ironically, the man responsible for it was Scottish, King James, the sixth of Scotland, and the first of England. Though the vernacular languages of Europe were beginning to develop a literary prose, what hope was there for Scots with this triumphant proof that God spoke English? Now, three hundred years later, the late Mr Lorimer's translation, completed after his death by his son, has arrived to show that Scots is up to the challenge.

Here is a remarkable parallel with the situation in Palestine from the third century B.C. to the second century A.D. In each case a powerful translation of the Scriptures, the Septuagint and the Authorized Version respectively, produced in the language of the dominant power, affected the spoken vernacular. The Aramaic survived, in popular speech, much better than did the Scots, but the period which elapsed before versions were produced in the vernacular in these two instances was remarkably similar.

This example from Scots/English is a further demonstration of the nature of bilingualism, in addition to the illustrations given in the text of this work from Welsh/English and German/English. Further analogies can be given from Spanish/English.

Mrs H. is an American bilingual daughter of Mexican-American bilingual parents. The parents have lived almost the whole of their lives in bilingual situations, whereas the daughter, married to an American monoglotic physician, lives in a monoglotic area. In lengthy discussions with the present writer, Mrs H. reiterated that "Spanishisms" came through in both the spoken and written English of her parents, and she gave numerous examples to support this contention.

Mrs T. is an American daughter of a Mexican-American bilingual mother, and a monoglotic American father. Mrs T.'s expertise in Spanish is more limited than that of Mrs H., but she emphatically confirmed Mrs H.'s contention that "Spanishisms" came through in her own mother's speaking and writing. She commented that this was especially noticeable in her mother's speech as she grew tired, in spite of the fact that the mother had lived most of her adult, married life in a part of the United States of America where Spanish-speaking people were very few.

On the basis of these conversations, the opportunity arose for the present writer to conduct an experiment in Spanish-English writing; in other words, to put to an empirical test the hypothesis that it was difficult to distinguish between a piece of prose written in a first language and then translated into a second, from a piece of prose written directly in a second language. Mr J. is an American university graduate, in his mid-twenties, who speaks fluent Spanish, having learnt the language at school, roomed with Spanish-speaking colleagues and spent vacations in Spanish-speaking countries. His close friend Miss C. is a native of Colombia in South America, whose native language is Spanish. She is a graduate of American universities and is extremely fluent in English, with an exceptionally wide English vocabulary. She has lived for several years in a predominantly monoglotic part of the U.S.A.

Both Mr J. and Miss C. agreed to undertake the following test:—

They each wrote a piece of prose in their native language, and then translated it into their second language; that is, Mr J. wrote a piece in English and translated it into Spanish, whilst Miss C. wrote in Spanish and then translated into English. Mr J. then wrote a second piece directly in Spanish, and Miss C. did the same in English. They then exchanged their pieces of prose to see if either could tell which piece had been written in their native language, and then translated, and which piece had been written directly in their second language. The results were most interesting. Miss C., who had by far the greater experience of bilingualism, could not distinguish between the two pieces which Mr J. had written. On the other hand, Mr J. was able to tell which piece of prose Miss C. had written in Spanish and translated into English, and which piece she had written directly in English.

Mr J. immediately volunteered his own interpretation of this phenomenon. He said that he knows, so thoroughly, how Miss C. thinks, and how she would approach such a task. Whilst both Mr J. and Miss C. are highly intelligent, extremely articulate and very well-educated people, Mr J.'s approach to life appears to be much more analytical than Miss C.'s. He implied that without his close personal knowledge of Miss C.'s way of thought he most probably would not have been able to distinguish between her two pieces of prose.

Another example, a recent experience, may be given. The present writer was in the home of Mrs A., who came to England from Finland over half a century ago, and married an English clergyman. Although her speech still has a Finnish accent, it is as grammatically correct as that of most of the people of the village in which she lives. Discussing the heating of her house, she produced a copy of a letter she had written to the Gas Board. It was she who pointed out that whilst the construction of her sentences in speech now followed the current English practice, her written sentence construction showed unmistakable signs of her native language, despite the fact that she had long experience of writing English in letters to her children who lived abroad.

APPENDIX C

Aramaic Words as used in the Gospels

word	Mark	Matthew	Luke	John
Abba	In Gethsemane	No mention	No mention	No mention
Bar	Only within the circle of the Disciples	As in Mark	As in Mark	No mention
Boanerges	The calling of the Disciples	No mention	No mention	No mention
Cephas	No mention	No mention	No mention	1.42
Gehenna	In reply to John	Sermon on Mount To the Disciples In Woes to Scribes and Pharisees	To the Disciples	No mention
Mammon	No mention	Sermon on Mount	To the Disciples	No mention
raca	No mention	Sermon on Mount	No mention	No mention
sata	No mention	Kingdom of Heaven parable	In synagogue	No mention
Rabbi	No mention	Title rejected by Jesus	No mention	No mention
Beelzebul	No mention	To Disciples (x.25) Introduced by Pharisees and used in reply by Jesus	Introduced by Pharisees and used in reply by Jesus	No mention
Satan	Temptations In Beelzebul controversy To Peter (Caesarea Philippi) In Parable of the Sower	Temptations In Beelzebul controversy To Peter (Caesarea Philippi)	Temptations In Beelzebul controversy To Peter (Last Supper) On return of the Seventy	No mention
Sabbath	To Pharisees, after they introduced it, and in a synagogue	To Pharisees, after they introduced it, and in a synagogue	To Pharisees, after they introduced it, and in a synagogue In the house of a Pharisee (xiv. 3 & 5)	In the Temple (vii.32)

APPENDIX D

The Word "Ephphatha"

The question could be asked why there has been no mention, much less any discussion, of the word *ephphatha* in the text of this work. This word is used only once in the Bible, in Mark vii. 34, but it is certainly there spoken by Jesus as part of the healing process of the deaf-mute. The reason why no reference has yet been made to this word is that the discussion in the main text was of the Aramaic words listed by Jeremias as those used by Jesus. Jeremias does not include the word *ephphatha* in his list.

The reason given for this omission by Jeremias is that there is some considerable uncertainty as to whether the word is Aramaic or Hebrew. In Young's Analytical Concordance the word is listed as Aramaic, coming from the Chaldean. In the commentaries on the Gospel according to St Mark, referred to above, Vincent Taylor and C.E.B. Cranfield state their agreement with Young. D.E. Nineham does not comment upon the language of this word. A.E.J. Rawlinson (Westminster Commentaries, 1925. p. 102), agrees that the word is Aramaic, and adds that "The use of the word in a latinised form (Effeta), accompanied by an application of saliva to the ears and nose of the candidate, came eventually to form part of the ceremonial of Baptism according to the usage of the Western Church (the so-called *aurium apertio*)."

Jeremias, in note 4, p. 7 of *New Testament Theology*, says:

> The thesis of I. Rabinowitz, supported by much learning, that *ephphatha* is Hebrew, because Palestinian Aramaic would not have assimilated the *t* to the *p*...is

expressly rejected by M. Black. He calls attention to examples of this assimilation in the Targum .... The judgement of J. A. Emerton is rather more restrained.... He concedes that *ephphatha* could be Hebrew, but leaves open the possibility that Galilean Aramaic made the assimilation in everyday speech.

Whatever the majority judgement upon this word, it makes no difference to the argument found in this work, for it has never denied Jesus' use of Aramaic, or the possibility of his knowledge of Hebrew. Although the healing apparently takes place on the borders of the Decapolis, there is no indication in S[t] Mark as to whether the man came from an Aramaic, a Greek-speaking or a bilingual background. As a deaf-mute he may have known no language. As "his ears were opened" after the word *ephphatha* was spoken, as far as the man was concerned, the language in which the healing words were spoken had no particular relevance. Two things emerge, however, from this brief discussion. The first is that the statement "Aramaic experts disagree amongst themselves" is seen here to be amply justified. The second point is that even in this disagreement, conjecture plays a major part.

Perhaps it would be appropriate to make a brief reference here to another "word" of Jesus, about which there is disagreement amongst scholars of Hebrew and Aramaic. This concerns the cry from the Cross, for in Mark xvi. 34 the words are recorded as "Eloi, Eloi, lama sabachthani," whereas in Matthew xxvii. 46, they are recorded as "Eli, Eli, lama sabachthani." (However, W. C. Allen, in his commentary on S[t] Matthew, transliterates the opening words as "Elei, Elei," although he does not say why he thus differs from the "Eli, Eli" used by both the Nestle and the Souter texts.) In respect of the Matthean text, Nestle notes some textual variations, in that both the fourth-century manuscripts Vaticanus and Sinaiticus have the "Eloi, Eloi," of S[t]

Mark, though this is probably due to assimilation.

It seems generally agreed that Mark's version is Aramaic, but somewhat Hebraized. Matthew's version is a more thoroughly Hebraized version. However, Vincent Taylor suggests that the cry was more probably uttered in Hebrew, for the comment of the bystanders, "He is calling for Elijah" would make more sense if this was so. However there are three points against accepting Taylor's view. First, it is entirely hypothetical; secondly there is no textual evidence to support this theory; and thirdly, few of the crowd would understand the Hebrew.

Jeremias has little comment to make upon this point, for he believes that Jesus was quoting Psalm xxii. The basis for this conviction is that he claims that this is the only time in the Gospels where Jesus uses the word "God" in prayer. However, as has been pointed out above, it would be natural, in this context, for Jesus to use Aramaic.

REFERENCES

Place of publication is London unless otherwise stated. Frequently cited works are referred to by the author's surname after first citation.

The Bible is quoted from the Revised Standard Version unless otherwise stated.

CHAPTER I

1 Edward Schillebeeckx, *Jesus, an Experiment in Christology*, New York, 1981, pp. 98 ff.
2 J. A. T. Robinson, *Can We Trust the New Testament?*, Oxford, 1977, p. 31
3 Jan H. Negenman, *New Atlas of the Bible*, 1969, p. 36
4 T. Boman, *Hebrew Thought compared with Greek*, 1960, p. 17
5 C. A. Briggs, *New Light on the Life of Jesus*, Edinburgh, 1904, pp. 134 ff.
6 X. Léon Dufour, *The Gospel and the Jesus of History*, 1968, p. 163
7 W. F. Howard, quoted from Moulton's Grammar by Vincent Taylor: see note 8.
8 Vincent Taylor, *The Gospel according to St Mark*, 1952, p. 55
9 W. C. Allen, *I.C.C. Commentary on St Matthew*, Edinburgh, 1959, p. 309

CHAPTER II

10 J. Jeremias, *New Testament Theology*, vol. 1, *The Proclamation of Jesus*, 1971
11 Allen, p. 49
12 Jeremias, p. 9
13 Jeremias, p. 11
14 Jeremias, p. 14
15 Jeremias, pp. 13 and 14
16 Jeremias, p. 14
17 Jeremias, p. 16
18 Jeremias, p. 23
19 Jeremias, p. 27
20 Jeremias, p. 26
21 Jeremias, p. 27
22 Jeremias, p. 196
23 Taylor, p. 56

CHAPTER III

24 E. M. Meyers and J. F. Strange, *Archeology, the Rabbis and Early Christianity*, Nashville, 1981, p. 73
25 *Ibid.*, p. 74

REFERENCES

26 The Mishnah, translated by Herbert Danby, Oxford, 1933, pp. xx ff.
27 *Ibid.*, pp. xiv ff.
28 R. McCrum, W. Cran, and R. MacNeil, *The Story of English*, 1986, p. 56
29 *Ibid.*
30 John xix. 19 ff.
31 A. D. Momigliano, "Greek Culture and the Jews", in M. I. Finlay (ed.), *The Legacy of Greece*, Oxford, 1984, chapter 11
32 Momigliano, p. 328
33 J. Bright, *A History of Israel*, 1964, p. 395
34 M. Noth, *The History of Israel*, 1960, p. 394
35 Momigliano, p. 328
36 Momigliano, p. 330
37 Momigliano, p. 331
38 Momigliano, pp. 357 ff.
39 N. Avigad, *Discovering Jerusalem*, Oxford, 1980, p. 75
40 Avigad, p. 81
41 Avigad, p. 85
42 Avigad, p. 106
43 Avigad, pp. 193 ff.
44 Avigad, p. 94
45 J. Finegan, *Light from the Ancient Past*, Princeton, 1947, p. 223
46 *Ibid.*, and Negenman, *New Atlas of the Bible*, illustration III
47 Meyers and Strange, p. 65
48 Meyers and Strange, p. 82
49 A. Dihle, "The Graecio-Roman Background", in H. J. Schultz (ed.), *Jesus in His Time*, 1971, p. 10
50 Meyers and Strange, p. 108
51 Dihle, p. 17
52 *Ibid.*
53 G. Bornekamm, *Jesus of Nazareth*, 1969, p. 54
54 Dufour, p. 118

CHAPTER IV

55 J. Stevenson, *A New Eusebius*, 1980, p. 52
56 C. Bigg, *The Origin of Christianity*, Oxford, 1909, p. 225
57 T. W. Manson, *The Sayings of Jesus*, 1950, p. 17
58 *Ibid.*, pp. 17 and 18
59 F. J. Foakes Jackson, *A History of the Christian Church*, Cambridge, 1905, p. 117
60 Manson, p. 17
61 B. J. Kidd, *A History of the Church to 461*, Oxford, 1922, p. 188
62 Manson, p. 11
63 Manson, pp. 11 ff.
64 Meyers and Strange, pp. 42 and 43
65 J. Barr, *Semantics of Biblical Language*, 1961, pp. 263 and 264
66 Manson, p. 14

67 C. J. Mullo-Weir, "The Biblical Languages: Hebrew & Aramaic", in T. W. Manson, *A Companion to the Bible*, 1947, p. 13
68 Meyers and Strange, p. 43
69 Noth, p. 422
70 A. Plummer, I.C.C. Commentary *The Gospel According to St Luke*, 1901, p. 174
71 G. S. Duncan, *The Epistle to the Galatians*, (Moffatt), 1934, p. 50
72 C. K. Barrett, *The Gospel according to St John*, 1955, p. 153
73 *Ibid.*, pp. 151 ff.
74 Robinson, p. 82

CHAPTER V

75 L. Rabinowitz, "The Synagogue and its Worship" in Manson, *A Companion to the Bible*, p. 457
76 W. O. E. Oesterley, "The Religious Background of the New Testament" in Charles Gore *et al.*, A New Commentary on Holy Scripture, 1929, Part III, p. 16
77 *Ibid.*
78 Meyers and Strange, pp. 140 and 141
79 Meyers and Strange, p. 141
80 Rabinowitz, p. 457
81 See D. S. Wallace-Hadrill, *Eusebius of Caesarea*, 1960, p. 63
82 E. W. Grinfield, *An Apology for the Septuagint*, 1850
83 R. H. Charles, *Between the Old and New Testaments*, 1931, p. 230. Although Jubilees, according to Charles, was written in Hebrew between 135 and 105 B.C., it follows the Septuagint in this respect.

CHAPTER VI

84 F. J. Foakes Jackson & Kirsopp Lake, *The Beginnings of Christianity*, 1933, vol. 4, p. 44
85 Cranfield, p. 4
86 A. R. Burn, *The Pelican History of Greece*, 1982, p. 367
87 *Ibid.*
88 C. F. Pfeifer, *The Dead Sea Scrolls and the Bible*, 1949, p. 44
89 J. Macdonald, *The Theology of the Samaritans*, 1964, p. 42
90 *Ibid.*, pp. 30 ff.

CHAPTER VII

91 J. A. T. Robinson, *The Priority of John*, 1985, p. 63
92 *Ibid.*, pp. 25 and 26

APPENDICES

93 N. Turner, "The Language of the New Testament", in Peake's Commentary on the Bible, 1962, pp. 659 ff.